Learn About Your Heart...
Made Simple

Editor-in-Chief
Nicolas W. Shammas
MS, MD, FACC, FSCAI

Illustrated by
Lynne Majetic, RN

Language Editor: Suzanne M. Hartung

Learn

About Your Heart...

Made Simple

First published in the United States in 2004 by
Midwest Cardiovascular Research Foundation
US BankCenter
201 West Second St., Suite 710
Davenport, Iowa 52801
Phone: 563.324.2828, Fax: 563.324.2835
Website: www.mcrfmd.com

ISBN 0-9755384-0-3
Distributed in the USA by:

Midwest Cardiovascular Research Foundation
US BankCenter, 201 West Second St., Suite 710
Davenport, Iowa 52801
Phone: 563.324.2828, Fax: 563.324.2835

Designer/Illustrator: Lynne Majetic, RN
Language Editor: Suzanne M. Hartung
Printer: MGM, East Moline, IL

To my lovely wife, Gail,
and my children,
WJ, Andy and Anna,
for their unconditional support.

To my parents for being there for me
whenever I needed them
and for their endless care and love.

Table of Contents

 # Preface

Learn About Your Heart . . . Made Simple is one
of the most exciting projects undertaken by the Midwest
Cardiovascular Research Foundation (MCRF). This book,
directed toward the general public, fulfills the Foundation's
main mission: improving the longevity and quality of life of
people in the communities we serve by fighting our No. 1
killer, heart disease.

The explosive knowledge about diseases of the heart
and blood vessels has made it difficult for many patients and
healthcare providers to keep up with this rapidly changing
field of medicine. The lay public is in the middle of these
rapid changes and quite often is exposed to complex,
confusing and sometimes misleading information. As a
practicing cardiologist, I often find myself spending more and
more time conveying current knowledge and undoing many
widespread misconceptions. I have come to realize that there
is a definite need for a comprehensive, unbiased and simple
heart and blood vessel book directed toward patients and the
general public.

Midwest Cardiovascular Research Foundation was
established in August 2002. Armed with an ambitious agenda
and dedicated, experienced staff, the Foundation launched
its project ***Learn About Your Heart . . . Made Simple***. With
16 contributing authors and 21 chapters spanning the major
aspects of heart and blood vessel diseases, the Foundation

offers a simple but comprehensive resource to the patients and the lay public. The book was written in question-and-answer format with a detailed index to help readers go directly to the questions they have in mind. This book is intended to assist readers in communicating more effectively with their healthcare providers, not as a substitute for medical attention.

We hope that this book will be a valuable resource to every individual who reads it, providing accurate knowledge about the function of the heart and blood vessels, the process by which disease develops, and the way it can be treated and prevented. Fighting heart and blood vessel diseases is not a one-time attempt but a continuous lifestyle change that will require discipline and a strong desire to change old habits and enhance one's quality of life. We hope that we have made it easier for readers, equipped with accurate information provided by this book, to move toward more healthful living.

Midwest Cardiovascular Research Foundation also is proud to present the local efforts of our community in fighting heart disease. Midwest Cardiovascular Research Foundation, the Quad-City Health Initiative (QCHI), the American Heart Association, the Quad-City medical societies in Iowa and Illinois, and the various medical centers and associations in our community best exemplify this local effort. These organizations have been very active in educating our community about health issues and have been strong fighters against the various risk factors of heart disease. We believe the model of cooperation between our regional Foundation and these local community initiatives will help translate the written knowledge of this book into immediate, real-life applications. The Foundation intends to take this model to its affiliates across the Midwest, hoping to achieve a larger cooperation and a more effective fight against heart disease.

The Foundation is indebted to the generous support we have received from the various foundations in our community that allowed this book to be distributed free of charge in the Quad City area. As we look forward to duplicating this effort in other communities, the general public will be able to access the contents of this book that will be posted periodically on our web page at www.mcrfmd.com. We are also indebted to the tireless efforts of many individuals who have made this book a reality by providing a high level of expertise, passion and dedication. I would like to acknowledge in specific Suzanne Hartung, the Language Editor; Shari Lemke, the Executive Research Administrator; Lynne Majetic, the Foundation's Medical Illustrator; and Maureen Koepke, the Executive Administrative Assistant of MCRF. Also, a special thanks to the Foundation's officers Dr. Eric Dippel (Secretary), and Mr. Richard Bittner (Treasurer), and to Mr. Steve Landauer.

We thank all those who support us and those who believe in the mission of our foundation. MCRF is a nonprofit 501 (c) 3 public charitable foundation. All donations are tax-deductible. If you wish to contribute to MCRF, please contact the Foundation office at 563.324.2828 or by email at koepkem@mcrfmd.com.

Nicolas W. Shammas, MS, MD, FACC, FSCAI
President and Research Director
Midwest Cardiovascular Research Foundation

 **Chapter 1**

Statistics about Heart and Blood Vessel Diseases in the United States

Nicolas W. Shammas, MS, MD, FACC, FSCAI

What is heart disease?

"Heart disease" is a nonspecific term that includes all problems that affect the blood vessels, the muscle, and the electrical system of the heart.

---

*Heart disease remains the No. 1 killer
in the United States.*

The heart muscle requires an uninterrupted oxygenated blood supply in order to survive and continue to function normally. Blockages in the *coronaries* of the heart can reduce the blood supply to the heart. Fatty deposits called *plaque* generally cause these blockages. The interruption of the blood supply to the heart can be a sudden process with rupture of those plaques and the formation of a blood clot inside the blood vessel. This sudden interruption of the blood supply leads to a *heart attack*, or damage to the heart muscle.

How frequent is heart disease in the United States?

According to the National Center for Health Statistics, the number of adults in the United States with the diagnosis of cardiovascular disease is about 64.4 million people, or 22.6% of the total population.

Heart disease remains the No. 1 killer in the United States, costing our health care budget approximately $360 billion annually. More than half of all deaths are attributed to heart and blood vessel diseases.

Heart disease alone accounted for approximately 930,000 deaths in 2001, claiming the life of one person every 34 seconds. Although men are more likely to be told that they have coronary artery disease than women, *heart disease is the No. 1 killer of women*.

Heart disease is more prevalent with age and coexists in significant percentages of patients with documented history of stroke or blockages in the blood vessels that supply the lower legs or the brain.

Ethnicity also seems to play a role in the prevalence of heart disease. The incidence of heart disease in Native Americans (Indians) or Alaskan Natives was about 12%, compared to 9% in Black adults and 5% in Asians. White adults have an incidence of heart disease of approximately 11%.

Families with income below poverty level have been reported to have a higher incidence of heart disease than adult members of families with higher incomes.

What are the statistics of coronary disease in the United States?

In the United States, approximately 900,000 people a year have a heart attack. There are approximately 400,000 people who will die from their heart attack before they reach a hospital or in the emergency room. This translates to about 1,095 Americans each day.

What is "sudden cardiac death"?

Sudden cardiac death occurs when electrical instability in the bottom chambers of the heart leads to a disorganized heart rhythm that renders the heart ineffective in pumping blood. If this electrical disturbance is not corrected within minutes of its occurrence, the victim of the heart attack dies.

What is a stroke?

A *stroke* occurs when the blood supply to a part of the brain has been interrupted. Brain cell death occurs. Strokes can be caused by a blockage to the artery of the brain *(ischemic)* or by a bursting of one of the arteries in the brain *(hemorrhagic)*. By far the most common types of strokes are ischemic strokes.

How frequent are strokes in the United States?

Over 750,000 strokes occur in the United States every year. Stroke is the third leading cause of death after heart attacks and cancer. A third of patients who experience strokes are younger than 65 years of age.

Plaques that obstruct blood to the blood vessels of the brain cause 35% to 40% of strokes.

3

About 20% of strokes are caused by irregularity in the heartbeat that affects the top chambers (atria) of the heart. This is referred to as *atrial fibrillation*.

The younger the individual with a stroke, the more likely that a hole in the heart *(called patent foramen ovale or atrial septal defect)* has been a contributing cause. It is estimated that 25,000 to 100,000 strokes a year might be attributed to this hole in the heart that separates the upper chambers of the heart.

Over 4.4 million people in the United States live with a stroke, and many of them have major disabilities.

What is heart failure?

Heart failure can be due either to weakness in the heart muscle or excess stiffness in the heart muscle. This results in an increase in the pressure inside the heart chambers leading to fluid in the lungs or the legs. The heart failure patient experiences fatigue, shortness of breath, occasional chest pain and lack of energy to perform basic activities.

What are the statistics about heart failure in the United States?

The American Heart Association and the American College of Cardiology have classified heart failure into four stages.

Stage A: There are about 60 million people in the U.S. with a normal heart who are at risk of developing heart failure.

Stage B: Ten million people have weakness in their heart muscle, but no symptoms.

Stage C: There are about 5 million people who are symptomatic with activity because of weakness in their heart muscle.

Stage D: This is the most advanced stage of heart failure. In this stage, the patient experiences shortness of breath even when resting. There are over 250,000 people in this stage in the United States.

What are risk factors for heart disease?

Risk factors for heart failure include the presence of coronary artery disease, high blood pressure (hypertension), diabetes, or a genetic tendency. Excess consumption of alcohol and the use of certain drugs also can weaken the heart muscle.

How is life expectancy among heart patients determined?

The strength of the heart muscle is a very strong predictor of a person's survival. The weaker the heart, the shorter is the life expectancy.

About 50% of the patients with heart failure might die within five years of their diagnosis. A third of patients who are alive with heart failure are rehospitalized within three months. *The overall cost of treating heart failure patients is twice that of all forms of cancer.*

The life expectancy of patients with heart failure is generally worse than for patients with cancers of the lung, breast, or colon.

What is hypertension?

Hypertension is *high blood pressure*. Blood pressure has 2 components. In a person with normal blood pressure, the top pressure *(systolic)* should be less than or equal to 130 mmHg (or less than 125mmHg in diabetics) and the bottom pressure *(diastolic)* should be less than 90 mmHg. When the blood pressure exceeds any of these numbers, a patient is then said to have hypertension.

How prevalent is hypertension in the United States?

There are approximately 15 million patients with high blood pressure in the United States. Unfortunately, the statistics indicate that in many people suffering from high blood pressure, physicians are not addressing the problem and treating their hypertension aggressively enough.

24% of Black people have been told that they have high blood pressure, compared to 20% of White adults and 14% of Hispanics.

Blood pressure incidence increases substantially with age. About 65% of people over the age of 60 have high blood pressure, in contrast to 30% of patients between the age of 40 and 59, and 7% of patients between the age of 18 and 39.

Why is treating hypertension important in preventing heart disease?

Hypertension is a major risk factor for strokes and heart attacks. Also, hypertension increases the risk for heart failure. More than 85% of heart failure patients have been diagnosed previously with high blood pressure or the presence of coronary disease. A third of men and women have high blood pressure as the main cause of their heart failure. Also, most patients with blockages in their coronaries or who have diabetes also have high blood pressure.

The lifetime risk of developing high blood pressure is about 90%. *Lowering blood pressure can reduce the incidence of stroke by about 35% to 40%, heart attacks by 20% to 25% and heart failure by about 50%.*

What is peripheral vascular disease?

Peripheral vascular disease is defined as blockages in the blood vessels of the body except those that supply the heart or the brain. Since all blood vessels in the body are part of the same vascular tree, blockages in the periphery are similar in nature to the coronaries or the arteries of the brain.

What is the prevalence of peripheral vascular disease in the United States?

This condition is very prevalent in the United States. Approximately 10 million people live with peripheral vascular disease. Half of them have no symptoms, and only a small percentage of them are being treated (12.5%). Over 700,000 patients receive treatment with either medications or nonsurgical procedures. Approximately 500,000 receive surgical treatment.

The incidence of peripheral vascular disease increases with age. One percent of patients over the age of 55 will experience a critical reduction in the blood flow to their lower legs.

The presence of peripheral vascular disease generally indicates a higher risk of mortality in the future. Over 60% of males and 30% of females with peripheral vascular disease will die by ten-year follow-up.

There is a considerable overlap between the presence of blockages in the blood vessels of the periphery, the heart, and the brain. In fact, patients who have documented blockages in their peripheral vasculature are at four times greater risk of heart attacks and two to three times greater risk of strokes.

The relative five-year mortality from severe peripheral vascular disease exceeds that of breast cancer, colon, and rectal cancer, as well as certain types of lymphoma.

How serious a problem is obesity in the United States?

Obesity refers to either an increase in weight of more than 20% above normal weight for gender, age and height or a Body Mass Index of 30 or more. The *Body Mass Index* (or *BMI*) is determined by the weight in kilograms divided by the square of the height in meters.

Obesity is one of the fastest-growing health concerns in the United States. 58 million people in the United States are overweight and 40 million are obese.

Eight out of ten people over the age of 25 are overweight.

Obesity also has affected children in the United States and is reaching epidemic proportions. In 2001, over one-quarter of all White children and a third of Black and Hispanic children were categorized as overweight.

Associated with this epidemic is a rise in several health problems including diabetes, heart disease, breast and colon cancer, and high blood pressure.

The cost of obesity-related diseases in the United States is staggering. Over $70 billion annually is spent on the treatment of diabetes, high blood pressure, and heart disease, all of which are related to obesity.

Lack of activity in the United States accounts substantially toward obesity. A quarter of Americans are completely sedentary. Approximately 78% of Americans do not meet recommendations for basic activity level.

What is diabetes?

Diabetes mellitus – elevated blood glucose – is a disease related to the inability of the body to use sugar effectively. Insulin, a hormone that the pancreas makes, facilitates blood sugar to be taken up by the tissues. Diabetes mellitus occurs when the pancreas is not capable of making enough insulin or when resistance to insulin is present.

How prevalent is diabetes in the United States?

In the United States, 18.2 million people have diabetes, which is approximately 6.3% of the population.

There are 260,000 people under the age of 20 who have diabetes, which represents 0.25% of the people in this age group.

Diabetes is on the rise in children primarily because of obesity and sedentary lifestyle.

18.3% of all people over the age of 60 have diabetes, which represents about 8.6 million people.

11.4% of Blacks over the age of 20 and 8.4% of Whites and Hispanics over the age of 20 have diabetes.

American Indians tend to have a higher incidence of diabetes mellitus, almost 2.3 times more as Whites.

Diabetes is the sixth leading cause of death in the United States in the year 2000, and the risk of dying in people with diabetes is twice that of non-diabetics.

The cost of diabetes in United States in 2002 was a staggering $132 billion.

What are the cigarette-smoking statistics in the United States?

In the United States, approximately 1 out of 4 men and 1 out of 5 women are smokers. This incidence is substantially higher among American Indians and Alaskan Natives.

Among males, 25% of Whites, 27.6% of Blacks, and 23.2% of Hispanics are smokers.

Among women, 21.7% of Whites, 18% of Blacks, and 12.5% of Hispanics smoke.

The prevalence of smoking decreases with higher years of education and with higher economic status.

90% of new smokers started as teenagers.

Currently there are more people quitting smoking. In

1991, 27% of Americans smoked, in contrast to 1964, when 44% of the population smoked.

Although more people are quitting smoking, unfortunately there continues to be a large number of people who become smokers. In the United States, smoking is responsible for 440,000 deaths each year. Since 1996, state-specific smoking rates have not declined significantly.

It should be also noted that *mortality continues to be substantially high in smokers who reduce their daily tobacco but do not quit entirely. Stopping smoking completely is a "must" to reduce mortality.*

Women who smoke and take birth control pills are 39 times more likely to have a heart attack and 20 times more likely to suffer from a stroke.

80 billion dollars per year are spent in the United States on health costs related to smoking.

How does others' smoking affect non-smokers?

"Passive smoking" ("second-hand smoke") continues to increase the risk of coronary artery disease substantially in both men and women.

What is congenital heart disease?

Congenital heart disease represents more than 35 different types of heart defects that persist after birth. Various defects have to do with abnormal connections between the chambers of the heart or abnormalities in the great blood vessels or valvular structure of the heart. Less frequent defects involve the actual chambers of the heart.

What are the statistics on congenital heart defects in the United States?

According to the American Heart Association, about one million Americans are alive today with congenital heart defect. There were about 4000 Americans who have died from those defects in 2001.

The death rates in 2001 per 100,000 people for heart defects were 1.6 for White males and 1.4 for White females and 2 for Black males and 1.6 for Black females.

There has been a substantial decline in the death rate from heart defects in the United States over the past ten years by about 28%.

A large proportion of congenital heart defects can be corrected either by minimal invasive surgery or by a full surgical procedure. Survival depends significantly on the type of the defect and the time between its diagnosis and correction.

Making changes to improve your heart health

While these statistics indeed are sobering, there are positive steps we all can take to improve our heart health.

It is never too late to make positive changes in your life.

In this book we address the most frequently asked questions about heart disease and provide you with unbiased answers. We hope these answers will help you change your life in a positive way to improve your heart health and to live a fuller, longer and more satisfying life.

 **Chapter 2**

Structure and Function of the Heart and Blood Vessels

Nicolas W. Shammas, MS, MD, FACC, FSCAI

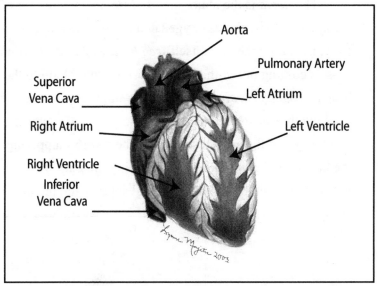

Figure 1. Heart with major external structures.

What is the function of the heart?

The heart is a pump that distributes blood to the organs of the body. The heart is made of 4 chambers. The top two collecting chambers are called *atria*; the bottom two ejecting chambers are called *ventricles* (*see Figure 1*).

13

The right atrium receives blood deficient in oxygen from the body and in return sends it into the right ventricle. The right ventricle squeezes the blood out to the lungs to pick up fresh oxygen. The oxygenated blood returns from the lungs to the left atrium, which then funnels the blood into the left ventricle. The left ventricle ejects the oxygenated blood to the entire body via the aorta.

What is the aorta?

The *aorta* is the major blood vessel that comes out of the heart and distributes oxygenated blood to the rest of the body, including the heart itself *(see Figures 2 and 3)*. Blood vessels coming out of the aorta and supplying blood to the heart are called *coronaries*. The aorta supplies blood to the head via the *carotid* and *vertebral* arteries. Major branches coming out of the aorta also include the *renals* (supplying the kidneys), the *mesenterics* (supplying the gut), the *celiac* artery (supplying the liver and spleen) and the *iliacs*

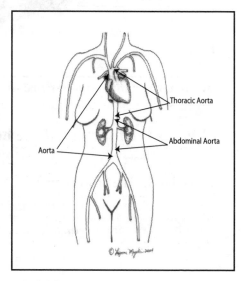

Figure 2.
The aorta is the major blood vessel that distributes oxygen-rich blood to the rest of the body.

14

(supplying the hip and lower legs). Diseases that affect the aorta and its branches are many but most commonly include cholesterol buildup with subsequent blockages, stretching and dilatation, called *aneurysms*, or tears, called *dissections*.

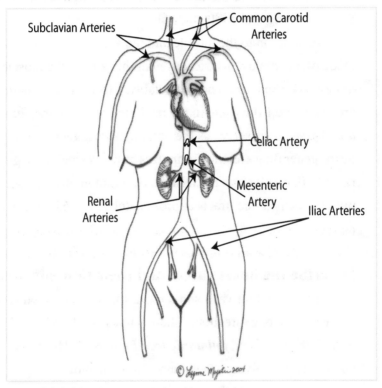

Figure 3. Major arteries that branch from the aorta.

What are the major components of the heart?

The heart is made of a contracting muscle that generates the force required to transport blood to all parts of the body. The muscle contracts from the bottom up to eject the blood into the aorta, the main blood vessel coming out of the heart. The aorta branches out into a network of blood vessels that distributes blood to the organs of the body.

In the heart, there are four valves that allow the blood to move in one direction only. For instance, the aortic valve opens up when the ventricle contracts and closes immediately when the heart relaxes, preventing the blood from returning to the left ventricle.

In addition to the muscle and the valves, the heart is made of a complex electrical system that allows the muscle to pump continuously and predictably. Electrical impulses are generated from a site in the right atrium called the *sino-atrial node*. This serves as the natural pacemaker of the heart, generating electrical impulses at the normal resting rate of 60 to 100 beats per minute. At a rate of 60 beats per minute, the heart contracts approximately 31,536,000 beats per year.

Describe the heart valves and their function

There are four valves in the heart that allow blood to move only in one direction. These valves are the *aortic*, *mitral*, *tricuspid* and *pulmonic (see Figure 4)*. The aortic and pulmonic valves, when open, allow the blood to leave the heart, and when closed, prevent the blood from returning to the heart. The mitral and tricuspid valves, when open, allow the blood to move from the atria to the ventricles, and when closed, prevent the blood in moving backward into the atria. A leak in one valve *(regurgitant)* indicates that the valve does not close well, allowing blood to move backward through it. A narrowed valve *(stenotic)* does not allow adequate blood to go through it when opened.

Endocarditis, an infection of the valves, can occur in patients with damaged or structurally abnormal valves. Endocarditis can damage the valves and is a condition that requires aggressive antibiotic therapy and occasionally urgent valve surgery.

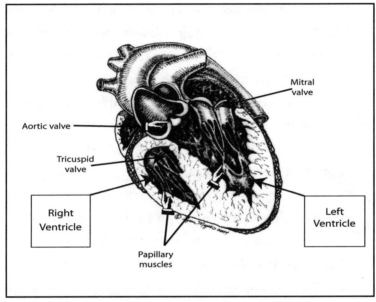

Figure 4. Heart valves. Pulmonic valve not pictured due to plane of dissection.

What are heart sounds and murmurs?

Heart sounds are generated from the closure of the valves. There are two normal heart sounds. One is generated from closure of the mitral and tricuspid valves when the heart contracts and is called S1. The second heart sound is generated from the closure of the aortic and pulmonic valves when the heart relaxes and is called S2.

Abnormal heart sounds can be generated in the setting of heart failure (S3) or from a very stiff ventricle such as in the setting of long standing high blood pressure or heart attacks (S4).

Heart murmurs can range from very normal (or ***physiologic***), in the setting of normal valvular function, to very abnormal (or ***pathologic***), such as in the setting of a leak *(regurgitation)* or narrowing *(stenosis)* in the valves. When a valve is narrowed, the blood ejected through it generates a high velocity jet and turbulence, which causes the murmur. Also, if a valve leaks, a high jet of blood flows through the leaky valve, generating a murmur. Murmurs have various characteristics and generally can tell a physician a lot of information about the function of the valves of the heart.

Heart sounds and murmurs are heard with a ***stethoscope*** placed over the heart, a process called ***auscultation***.

What are the arteries?

The heart pumps blood into the blood vessels, a series of pipes that take blood from the heart to the organs of the body (via the ***arteries***) and send the blood back into the heart (via the ***veins***). The arteries are muscular and elastic (like a rubber band) and are able to send the blood in a pulsatile form to all organs. As the arteries enter an organ, they branch and narrow significantly to reach all parts of this organ. Arteries expand as they receive blood from the heart and recoil back like the rubber band to aid in pushing the blood forward to the organs. Arteries carry oxygenated blood to all the organs except the lung. The *pulmonary artery* arises from the right ventricle and carries blood deficient in oxygen into the lung.

What are the veins?

Once the nutrients and oxygen are delivered to an organ, the blood needs to return to the heart to start the cycle over again. The *capillary* branches rejoin, forming larger, flexible vessels capable of holding blood. These collecting blood vessels are called *veins*. The small veins link up to become larger veins. The larger veins eventually lead back to the atria of the heart via the *inferior vena cava* (the main vessel carrying blood to the heart from the lower body) or the *superior vena cava* (the main vein carrying blood from the upper body, especially the head). Unlike the arteries, the vein has very little muscle layer. Also, one-way valves help the blood to flow in one direction toward the heart through the veins. Incompetence of these valves can lead to varicose veins and accumulation of fluid in the legs upon sitting or standing for long times.

What are the capillaries?

In the organs, the vessels become very small and their walls very thin. These tiny vessels are called *capillaries*. Across the capillaries, oxygen is exchanged between the blood and the organs. Also, these capillaries facilitate nutrient delivery and waste pickup. The capillaries are so thin and small that blood elements are forced to line up single file to pass though this vessel. At this scale, the individual blood cells pass into the capillaries like cars passing through a tollgate. Having regulators at the openings of the capillaries means that blood can be diverted and delivered to the organs in a quantity proportionate to the need of this organ. For instance, when someone is jogging, more blood is delivered to the muscles of the legs to meet the higher oxygen demands.

Describe the electrical system of the heart

The electrical system of the heart *(see Figure 5)* is made of a natural pacemaker called the ***sino-atrial node (SA node),*** which generates electrical impulses at the normal rate of 60-100 beats per minute. The SA node is located in the right atria. Once the SA node generates electricity, it is conducted across a wiring system from the atria down to the ventricles.

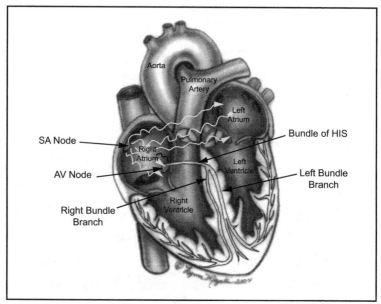

Figure 5. Electrical System of the heart.

At the junction of the atria and ventricle, the *atriventricular node (AV node)* is present and acts as a filter, allowing only a certain number of beats to reach the lower part of the heart. It protects the heart from excessive beats generated by the atria in certain disease states. The AV node also acts as a backup pacemaker in case the SA node fails. The AV node, however, generates lesser number of electrical impulses than the SA node at 50-60 per minute.

Once electricity crosses beyond the AV node, it is conducted to the bottom part of the ventricles via 2 major wires called the right (to the right ventricle) and left (to the left ventricle) *bundles*. Problems in these bundles lead to *heart blocks* that quite often require insertion of a permanent pacemaker. Heart blocks prevent electricity from reaching adequately the ventricles, slowing the heart beats considerably and leading to fainting or near-fainting spells.

What is an ECG?

An *ECG* or an *electrocardiogram* is a recording of the electrical impulse of the heart from the surface of the body. The ECG can tell a doctor whether the electricity of the heart is conducting normally or if there is an abnormality that warrants immediate attention. The ECG can also tell (but not all the time) whether a heart attack is acutely happening in a patient with chest symptoms. The ECG also can give clues to other structural problems in the heart and is an integral part of the evaluation of a potential heart patient.

What is the pericardium?

The **pericardium** is a sac in which the heart sits. It is not essential to the life of a person. However, it does have several useful functions, including limiting short-term distention of the heart and helps maintain the shape of the heart. It also facilitates the interaction between the chambers of the heart and serves as a mechanical barrier for infection. Furthermore, the pericardium helps lubricate the heart and minimizes friction. Other functions of the pericardium are beyond the scope of this book.

The pericardium can be affected by numerous disease states. The cavity between the heart and the pericardium is called the ***pericardial cavity***. This cavity can become filled with fluids after an infection, bleeding, trauma, tumors or other causes. The pressure generated from this fluid can compress the heart. Also, thickening of the pericardium can limit the heart expansion and causes ***constrictive*** disease. This can cause shortness of breath and worsening fluid in the lower legs. *(See Chapter 12 for a more detailed description of diseases of the pericardium.)*

 **Chapter 3**

Diseases of the Blood Vessels of the Heart

Nicolas W. Shammas, MS, MD, FACC, FSCAI

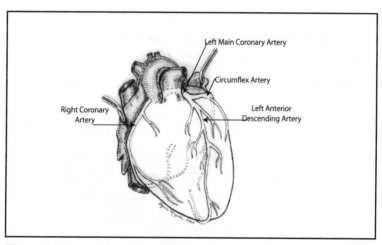

Figure 1. Heart with major coronary arteries.

How does the heart receive its blood supply?

The heart is a pump that continuously beats at 60 to 100 beats per minute during the life of a person. This pump requires oxygen and nutrients to achieve its tasks. These are delivered to the heart via blood vessels called the ***coronaries*** *(see Figure 1)*. There are three or four major coronary arteries that deliver blood to the heart. These supply the top (left anterior descending artery), the side (the left circumflex),

23

and the bottom (the right coronary artery) of the heart. Any interruption of blood supply to any of those coronaries can lead to heart damage to a correspondent part of the heart muscle.

How do the coronaries fill up with plaques and become obstructed?

The coronaries are covered on the inside by a lining called the ***endothelium*** *(see Figure 2),* a single layer of cells that covers every single blood vessel in our body. It has been estimated that if this lining of all the blood vessels from one individual is spread on a flat surface, it could cover two tennis courts in size. This single layer of cells, however, separates the blood vessels from health and disease.

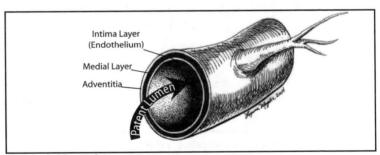

Intima Layer
(Endothelium)

Medial Layer

Adventitia

Patent Lumen

Figure 2. Normal Artery.

Any damage to the endothelium can lead to its invasion by blood elements called ***monocytes***. These monocytes penetrate under the lining of those blood vessels and absorb fat from the bloodstream. They become enlarged in size and are called ***foam cells***. These foam cells promote a complex reaction under the endothelium, which subsequently causes inflammation and attracts various other cells to the plaque area. The plaque expands and starts to impinge on the opening of the blood vessels that supply the heart *(see Figure 3)*.

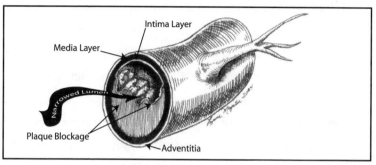

Figure 3. Artery with plaque build-up.

It is well-known that the process of plaque formation starts very early in childhood. Autopsies on young soldiers who died in wars have shown that the blood vessels of their bodies already show the buildup of fat under the endothelium. Over two-thirds of people over the age of 40 show the buildup of plaque in the blood vessels that supply their heart, as seen by ultrasound scanning of those blood vessels.

What is angina?

Angina is a symptom of chest pain – also described as chest pressure, a heavy feeling in the chest, a squeezing sensation in the chest – which is caused by a lack of blood supply to a part of the heart muscle. Angina is described as either stable or unstable.

A narrowing in one of the blood vessels of the heart by plaque build-up causes ***stable angina***. Stable angina occurs when a person is active and doing physical exertion.

25

It typically resolves within two to three minutes of resting. This type of angina does not occur at rest. As a person becomes active and exerts himself or herself, the heart has to pump faster and stronger. With the increase in the heart rate, there is a need to increase the blood supply to the heart to continue to match its demands. If plaque buildup is severe enough to narrow the coronaries, then the blood supply to the heart cannot increase at the rate needed by the heart. A mismatch of demand and blood supply occurs. This generates discomfort in the heart – angina. Once the patient rests and the demands of the heart for blood supply returns to normal, then the pain resolves.

In contrast to stable angina, a rupture of the plaque inside the blood vessels causes *unstable angina*. This leads to a subsequent accumulation of a clot at the area of the plaque rupture, which abruptly and partially interrupts the blood supply to the heart. Angina then occurs with very minimal activity or at rest. *This type of angina requires immediate medical attention.*

How does the patient perceive angina?

Angina is perceived as chest pressure, tightness, a squeeze, or heaviness in the chest. This could radiate to the arm and the jaw, the shoulders, the back, or the abdomen. The pain can be associated with an increase in shortness of breath, a feeling of nausea, and occasional vomiting. Also, patients break out in a sweat, which is called *diaphoresis*. Lightheadedness and anxiety accompany those symptoms. Patients might describe one or more of these symptoms, on many occasions, without any chest discomfort. Females and diabetics tend to present with atypical symptoms without chest pain.

What should you do if you experience chest pain or other symptoms of angina?

If you experience chest pain or any of the symptoms described on the preceding page, it is important that you do not attempt to self-diagnose. *It is very important in this situation to seek immediate medical attention.* If the pain occurs at rest, this is essentially an emergency and driving to the hospital or having someone to drive you can be very dangerous. The best way to deal with your *rest angina* is to **call 9-1-1** and allow paramedics to transport you to the hospital. The first hour of the onset of the chest discomfort is the most dangerous. Electrical disturbances in the heart can occur and the heart could cease pumping blood to the brain and the vital organs of the body. This can be easily corrected if you are being transported to the hospital with trained professionals. However, *sudden cardiac death* can occur if you are still at home or you are in a regular car on your way to the hospital. A sudden change in symptoms – such as the occurrence of nausea or vomiting, sudden worsening of breathing, or the occurrence of chest pain – all warrant immediate hospital evaluation.

If the chest pain or the anginal symptoms have been occurring primarily with exertion or activity, but never at rest, this tends to be somewhat less of an emergency. However, evaluation should be performed relatively soon. Calling your doctor and getting evaluated relatively soon is important. The symptoms of pain with exertion are classic anginal symptoms and they have a high chance to be related to obstructive plaque in the coronary arteries.

How does a patient die from a heart attack?

The most common cause of death from heart attack is electrical instability to the heart. Once the blood supply is interrupted, the electrical conduction inside the heart becomes disturbed. Abnormal electrical circuits are generated in the bottom chambers of the heart. These lead to quivering of the heart muscle. The heart muscle becomes very inefficient in pumping blood. These arrhythmias are called *ventricular tachycardia* or *ventricular fibrillation*. The blood will be able to generate minimal to no blood supply to the vital organs of the body, including the brain. A person loses consciousness usually within 5 to 10 seconds of the occurrence of this event. Death occurs if the electrical system of the heart is not restored back to its normal condition within 5 to 6 minutes of the electrical disturbance. Rarely, heart failure resulting from the heart attack leads to death. By far, the majority of deaths are related to this electrical instability. Paramedics and hospitals are equipped with machines called defibrillators that are capable of aborting those electrical heart rhythms by delivering an electrical shock to the chest. Automatic external defibrillators are now widely placed in public places such as airports, schools, and large business centers. Operation Heartbeat, a program of the American Heart Association, extends the use of automatic external defibrillators in public places in order to save lives of heart attack victims.

Cardiopulmonary resuscitation, which includes

artificial respiration and chest compression, can sustain enough of a blood circulation for the first 10 minutes after the electrical instability has occurred.

However, without the more definitive therapy of defibrillation using the defibrillator, cardiopulmonary resuscitation is inadequate alone to restore a normal heart rhythm. In fact, survival rate after six minutes of the arrhythmia is slim despite cardiopulmonary resuscitation and without defibrillation.

What does my doctor do when I come to the emergency room with chest pain?

Your doctor will evaluate you with a full history and physical exam. Details of the chest pain such as its onset, severity, radiation, and association with other symptoms or with activity will all be important information to provide. A physical exam to listen to your lungs and heart will be important. Based on all the information gathered, including blood testing, your physician will attempt to determine whether your symptoms could be related to your heart or are non-cardiac in origin.

If it is a possibility that these symptoms are heart-related, then you will be asked to stay in the hospital. Many hospitals have a chest pain unit where you will be observed on a monitor for several hours. Blood will be obtained at different intervals to rule out the possibility of heart injury. An electrocardiogram also will be obtained. Eventually, if all your tests are unremarkable (no "red flags"), a stress test will be performed.

All these tests will help your doctor to decide whether

to admit you to the hospital for further workup, such as a coronary angiogram. On the other hand, if your chest pain has occurred at rest and continues to do so in the emergency room, your doctor will have to assume that this is an unstable anginal symptom. You will then be directly admitted to the hospital and placed on medical treatment. If the suspicion for cardiac-related symptoms is high, then your doctor might proceed directly with an angiogram.

What is a cardiac catheterization, or a coronary angiogram?

A *cardiac catheterization* is essentially the same as a *coronary angiogram*. This procedure is performed in the cardiac catheterization laboratory. During this procedure, a small plastic tube is inserted in the blood vessels in the groin, called the *common femoral artery*. This small plastic tube or catheter is placed under a local anesthetic. Through this catheter, plastic tubes are placed inside the blood vessels under x-ray guidance. These go to the heart, where a contrast dye is injected. The dye is injected directly into the heart's chamber as well as in the blood vessels of your heart. As the dye is being injected into those blood vessels, an x-ray camera takes multiple pictures of your heart, which will allow your physician to see your coronaries and determine the location of the blockages, if present.

The angiogram is considered an invasive procedure. It does carry some risks with it. These risks vary depending on the condition of the patient. Patients with heart failure and reduced heart function, diabetes or kidney problems tend to be at exceptionally high risk. Patients with previous history

30

of heart attacks, strokes, and blockages in the blood vessels of the legs are also at higher risk. However, the overall risks of the procedure remain small. In a non-emergent angiogram, the risk of death should be less than 1 in a 1000, risk of strokes 1 in 500, and the risk of major bleeding from the insertion site of the catheter should be less than 1%. Obviously, these risks also vary if the angiogram is only for diagnostic purposes to identify the location of the blockage or for treatment purposes to treat the blockage.

During the treatment of blockages, large amounts of blood thinners are administered, which increases the risk of bleeding and complications. Other risks of the angiogram also include infection, damage to the nerves in the groin area, damage to the arteries of the heart themselves, as well as the aorta, the main artery that comes out of the heart and supplies blood to the rest of the body. Your doctor will weigh carefully all those risks compared to the potential benefits of the test.

Typically, an ***informed consent*** – a legal contract that authorizes the physician to proceed with the test – is obtained after you understand these risks and your questions and concerns are answered. Signing a consent form essentially acknowledges your understanding of these risks and your willingness to proceed with the test. You should treat it seriously, read it carefully, and feel free to ask any questions. The physician or the nurse should be available to answer any questions you might have to your satisfaction.

How do we treat blockages in the coronaries once they are found?

Blockages in the blood vessels of the heart are treated in three different ways.

1) Your doctor might decide that your coronary blockages are only borderline in nature or insignificant, and preventative therapy and medical therapy might be advised.

2) If your blockages, however, are severe, then the treatment can be done by either an **angioplasty** or a **bypass surgery**. During an angioplasty, your cardiologist passes a balloon into the blocked arteries. Once the balloon is inflated at the area of the blockage *(see Figure 4)*, the blockage will be compressed and the artery is stretched. A **stent**, or a stainless steel mesh, is most frequently deployed in the area of the treatment to keep the artery widely open and prevent it from collapse. The choice of the stent depends on the type of blockages, their location, and the ability to deliver the stent to that part of your coronaries.

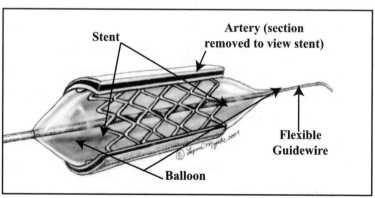

Figure 4. Stent, mounted on a balloon, being implanted in an artery.

Although the current standard of treating blockages is with the use of a stent, some blockages do not permit stenting because of their size or the difficulty of delivering the stents to a particular blockage because of blood vessel *twists and turns (tortuous)* and *calcification*. Current stents also have medications in them. These medications reduce the chance of recurrence of blockages within the area of the treatment. The choice of the stents is also guided by certain rules that your doctor might follow. Currently, the majority of the blockages are managed through the angioplasty process.

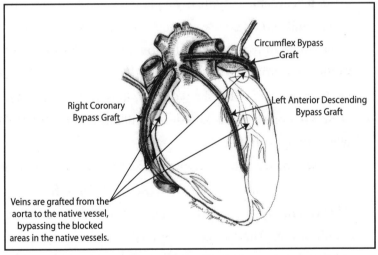

Figure 5. Heart with veins bypassing blocked coronary arteries.

3) However, some blockages might be in locations too dangerous or extensive to treat with an angioplasty procedure. They might be complex in nature, particularly if they occur in a diabetic. Currently, the trend is to treat those blockages with the *bypass operation*. During the bypass

operation, a blood vessel under the collarbone and/or a vein derived from under the skin of the legs are utilized to bypass the area of the blockage *(see Figure 5)*.

How long does it take to recover from the treatment of a blockage in the heart?

If an angioplasty is utilized as the primary method of treating a blockage, then generally you stay in the hospital for 23 hours. Within 72 hours, you should be able to drive and resume your normal activities.

The exception to this is if you have had a heart attack. After a heart attack, typically a patient cannot drive for two weeks and should be undergoing cardiac rehabilitation for a minimum of four weeks prior to release back to work or other normal daily activities. Your doctor will decide on the size of the heart attack that you had, the extent of cardiac rehabilitation required, and the optimal time for you to return to full daily activities.

On the other hand, bypass surgery would require that you stay in the hospital for an average of four to five days. This can be significantly more prolonged if complications would occur. The recovery phase is in the range of about six weeks. For about three months, you should avoid carrying any weight that exceeds 10 pounds, avoiding any form of exertion that would require pulling and pushing. It is also important to minimize any trauma to the area of the wound in the middle of the chest. Driving typically is not permitted during the first month after bypass surgery.

There are many exceptions to the above rules based on your condition, any complications that might have occurred during surgery, and your recovery.

What is the long-term outcome following treatment of blockages in the heart?

Following the treatment of a blockage with an angioplasty, there is an immediate inflammation that occurs at the site of the treatment. This response of the blood vessel to the injury that the balloon has caused triggers the formation of scar tissue at the site of the treatment. Patients develop scar tissue to a different extent for unclear reasons. The scar tissue that develops within the stent can potentially cause a recurrence of a blockage in the area of the treatment.

When balloon angioplasty alone was utilized without stenting, the recurrence of the blockage was in the range of about 40%. When a stent is used, the recurrence of a blockage is in the range of 15 to 20%.

Higher rate of recurrence occurs in diabetics, patients with small blood vessels, and those with long areas of blockages.

With the advent of the stents loaded with drugs that suppress these *blockages (drug-eluting stents)*, the rate of recurrence of scar tissue is currently about 5 to 9%.

It is typical for scar tissue to form within the first six months of an angioplasty. If this does not occur within the first six months, it is extremely less likely that it will occur afterwards.

Your doctor might elect to proceed with a stress test at about four to six months following an angioplasty to determine whether enough scar tissue has occurred to block the artery again. The decision to do this stress test is generally a clinical one and depends upon your doctor's recommendation.

The overall outcome of the patient, however, from the standpoint of preventing a heart attack, is mostly dependent on preventative measures rather than the angioplasty process itself. In other words, angioplasty for blockages that have caused no symptoms or only stable symptoms generally does not affect a person's survival. The major impact of angioplasty is on improving the quality of life and lessening the need for medications.

In order to prevent death or a heart attack long-term, strict control of cardiac risk factors becomes important. This includes controlling the blood pressure, cholesterol, blood sugar, the weight, and avoiding smoking. Dietary modification, exercise, and stress reduction also become very important. These will be covered in detail in the preventative chapter of this book.

Following a bypass surgery, the procedure's long-term success depends on the continued normal functioning of the bypass grafts. It is known that 10 to 15% of bypass grafts can deteriorate within the first year of surgery. Also, at about 10 years from a bypass, two-thirds of all bypasses are expected to have significant amount of build-up of plaques and blockages. There has been a lot of progress made recently in the treatment of those bypass grafts.

However, again, the overall long-term survival and benefit is highly dependent on preventative measures. Several studies have indicated that the viability of bypass grafts and their overall health is related to taking blood thinners, such as aspirin or clopidogrel, and the use of some cholesterol-lowering medications such as statins. Research is continually ongoing to find ways to preserve those bypasses and prevent them from deteriorating or blocking shortly after the surgery.

What is a heart attack and how does it happen?

Heart attack happens when there is a sudden interruption of the blood supply to a part of the heart muscle. This leads to death of the muscle tissue. A heart attack leads to symptoms similar to angina. However, these symptoms tend to be more prolonged and generally are more than a half-hour in duration. The interruption of the blood supply to the heart occurs because of a plaque rupture. A plaque, irrespective of severity, can break, exposing the inside of the plaque to the blood elements. The blood forms a clot on the top of the ruptured plaque. If the clot does not block the artery entirely, unstable angina certainly will occur, as described in previous questions. However, if the interruption in the blood supply is complete because of a full clot, then the muscle of the heart supplied by this particular blood vessel will be deprived of nutrients and oxygen and will die.

The most important step in the management of a heart attack is to restore the blood supply to the heart muscle as quickly as possible. The current guidelines strongly suggest that the artery should be opened with the angioplasty procedure within 90 minutes of a patient's arrival to the emergency room. If the angioplasty procedure is not available at this particular emergency room and hospital,

37

then the use of a clot-dissolving (or ***thrombolytic***) medicine needs to be used immediately, within 30 minutes of arrival to the emergency room. Many hospitals are able to initiate the use of these thrombolytic drugs within about 20 minutes of a patient arriving to the emergency room.

Current data strongly suggest, however, that the angioplasty is a more effective way of opening up an artery in a heart attack situation, and probably leads to a better short- and long-term outcome.

Therefore, it is imperative that when the pain starts or when symptoms of a heart attack start, the patient needs to be transported to an emergency room as soon as possible. Time is extremely precious and the longer the delay in opening a closed artery, the more damage will happen to the heart muscle. In fact, in four to six hours after the artery is closed, the damage is essentially complete. There is strong data to suggest that the earlier the artery is opened, the higher the likelihood of survival from a heart attack.

What medications should I expect to be on following a heart attack?

Following the acute treatment of a heart attack, which is primarily restoring the blood supply to the heart muscle, a patient is placed on several medications to reduce the chance of another heart attack and reduce mortality.

The standard therapy consists of the use of a beta-blocker that has been shown to reduce heart failure, arrhythmias, and prevent stretching and dilatation of the heart muscle following a heart attack.

In addition, the patient is expected to be on a ***statin***, which is a cholesterol-lowering medication that has also shown to substantially prevent the chance of another heart attack. The use of blood thinners such as aspirin and clopidogrel (Plavix) has become standard therapy to also reduce the chance of another cardiac event. The use of an *angiotensin-converting enzyme (ACE) inhibitor* in patients following a heart attack and reduced left ventricular function is also now a standard to prolong life and reduce the chance of further cardiovascular events.

With the use of a beta-blocker, an ACE inhibitor, aspirin, clopidogrel, and a statin, one would expect that the chance of recurrence of a heart attack should be reduced to less than 3% per year on this preventative therapy.

In addition to pharmacologic therapy, the patient will be strongly advised to watch strict dietary restrictions, weight control, exercise, and adhere to a no-smoking policy. All these changes require significant lifestyle modifications, which at times can be challenging. However, a patient striving for better health and to prevent another heart attack generally adheres to these guidelines.

How important is cardiac rehabilitation after a heart attack or a bypass surgery?

Cardiac rehabilitation in a structured format, with the patient being monitored, has been shown to improve substantially the quality of life with data also suggesting an improvement in survival. Cardiac rehabilitation allows patients to gain confidence in their ability to do things, gradually increases their fitness level, and helps them develop a habit to exercise routinely on a long-term basis.

The importance of exercise is mostly in its cardiovascular fitness and conditioning that allows a stronger ability of the body to extract oxygen from the blood, as well as improve the overall efficiency of the heart. A trained and fit individual tends to have a slower heart rate at rest and a lower adrenaline blood level. These are very protective elements overall to the heart.

Cardiac rehabilitation is very strongly recommended to cardiac patients after an angioplasty, a heart attack, or bypass surgery. A substantial number of patients see a tremendous improvement in their sense of well-being and an improvement in their depression after a heart attack. This, in itself, also has significant protective effect on their overall health as well as cardiovascular health.

The second phase of cardiac rehabilitation is the outpatient phase that follows a heart attack and is generally monitored under the guidance of cardiac rehabilitation nurses or technicians. The patient is generally placed on a monitor and different kinds of exercises are encouraged, with close monitoring of the heart rate and the blood pressure, as well as the heart rhythm. A gradual increase in the target heart rate is done under the guidance of the primary cardiologist.

The third phase of cardiac rehabilitation is a less-monitored phase where a person joins a group of heart patients and exercises on a routine basis. Phase III provides significant group support to the heart patient and allows uninterrupted, continued exercise with minimal supervision, but with some form of continued guidance.

 **Chapter 4**

Peripheral Vascular Disease

Eric J. Dippel, MD, FACC

What is Peripheral Vascular Disease (PVD)?

Peripheral vascular disease (PVD) is a term that describes blockages in the blood vessels that supply the entire body except the neck and head (called *cerebrovascular disease*) and the heart (called *coronary artery disease*).

Cholesterol not only clogs up the arteries of the heart, but it also clogs other arteries in the body. All of the arteries in the body are susceptible to this problem. The arteries to the neck are called the *carotid arteries* and they supply the head. When the carotid arteries become significantly blocked, patients are susceptible to stroke. This is explained more fully in Chapter 5.

The arteries to the kidneys, known as the *renal arteries*, also frequently become blocked. Typically, there are no symptoms associated with renal artery narrowing. However, since the kidneys are one of the organs that control your blood pressure, any sudden increase in your blood pressure might be a sign that your kidney arteries are becoming blocked.

Blockages can occur anywhere in the arteries to the

41

legs. When this occurs in a mild or moderate degree, the most common symptom is claudication, which is a "tight" or "tired" sensation in the leg muscles that occurs with walking and is relieved with rest *(see "What is Claudication?" below)*. When the blockages to the leg arteries become severe enough, then tissue in the leg begins to develop ulcers and die. If blood flow is not re-established promptly, then patients may require amputation of part of the leg.

What are the risk factors for peripheral vascular disease (PVD)?

The risk factors for PVD are identical to the risk factors of coronary artery disease (CAD): high cholesterol, cigarette smoking, diabetes, high blood pressure, obesity, and a family history of vascular disease. Since the arteries in our bodies become blocked up over time, PVD typically gets worse as people become older.

Since the risk factors for PVD and CAD are the same, many patients have both problems at the same time. Patients with PVD that is uncontrolled are more likely to die from heart attacks and strokes rather than from blockages in their lower legs.

Among the above risk factors, *smoking is the most hazardous for patients with PVD.* Quitting smoking not only reduces the risk of further disease, but also can be one of the most important interventions that can be done to reduce symptoms of pain in the lower legs.

How common is PVD?

PVD is quite common, although it is frequently under-recognized and under-diagnosed. A simple analogy is: when grandpa walks to the mailbox and gets chest pain, he is referred to the emergency room. However, when grandpa walks to the mailbox and his legs get tired, he simply is told he is "just getting old."

There are millions of Americans who have PVD, yet only a fraction actually receives treatment. Furthermore, there are thousands of amputations performed in this country every year that might be prevented if blockages obstructing the blood flow to the leg were detected and treated early. There are over 10 million people in the USA who live with peripheral vascular disease, but fewer than 25% are being treated. A higher index of suspicion is necessary for both patients and physicians to adequately search for, diagnose and treat PVD.

What is Claudication?

Claudication refers to the symptoms of leg fatigue and cramps that patients with PVD describe when they exert themselves. This is typically described as a "tight" or "cramping" sensation in the calves, thighs, or buttocks that occurs with walking. Typically, this occurs at a very predictable time in walking. For example, after walking one to two blocks, a patient would have to stop and rest.

Leg cramps at night while sleeping are typically not due to PVD. However, foot pain at night, along with discomfort in the calves with walking a short distance, can be a sign of very advanced PVD that would require immediate attention.

Advanced lack of blood supply to the lower extremities can result in skin ulceration, non-healing wounds and infection and ultimately tissue loss and amputations. ***Dependent rubor*** and ***elevation pallor*** are terms that describe advanced blockages in the arteries of the legs. When blockages are very severe, elevation of the legs leads to less blood supply to the foot that turns pale, and when the leg is dangled down, the foot turns red (gravity assisting the blood in reaching the feet). Patients sometimes complain of their feet and toes turning blue when dangled down. This is generally due to ***venous stasis***, or pooling of the blood to the lower legs, rather than insufficient blood reaching the toes.

What are the causes of leg pain?

Leg pain can be broken down into three major categories.

1. The first category is problems with blocked blood vessels and poor circulation. As described above, these symptoms of claudication occur with walking or exertion and are alleviated with rest. Patients can develop pain that occurs with rest only if the blockages are severe and the blood flow to the leg is extremely limited. Typically, if this occurs, there are other findings, such as discoloration of the skin or ulcerations of the foot, that go along with resting pain from poor circulation.

2. The second major type of leg pain is due to problems with the bones and joints, such as arthritis of the knees, ankles, and hips. This type of pain is typically worse

with standing and weight bearing on the joint. It may occur at rest and, not uncommonly, is improved with walking.

3. The third major type of pain is caused by nerve problems. For example, pinched nerves in the low back can cause sciatica pain which shoots down the hip and buttocks into the lower leg. This pain typically feels sharp and may be worse with certain positions. Another type of nerve pain is numbness and tingling of the feet that is frequently seen in diabetes. This has a sensation of "pins and needles" and may be present 24 hours a day.

What tests can be done to evaluate for PVD?

These tests can be broken down into noninvasive studies versus invasive studies. The simplest noninvasive study is simply by measuring the blood pressures in the arms and comparing it to the blood pressure in the legs. This is known as the *ankle/brachial index (ABI)*. The blood pressure in the ankles should be roughly the same as the blood pressure in the arms. If the ankle blood pressure is significantly decreased, then this is evidence that there are blockages somewhere in the legs. Pictures of the arteries in the legs can be obtained through either a CT scan or an MR scan. While these images are similar, for technical reasons, the CT scan probably provides more accurate images. Doppler ultrasound can also be used to measure blood flow into the arteries. This test is most commonly used to monitor the adequacy of blood flow through bypass grafts, but also can be utilized to assess the flow to the native arteries.

Invasive studies include the angiogram test. During this test, a catheter is placed in the arm or leg (at the groin level) under local anesthetic and contrast dye is injected through it to visualize the arteries.

What is the treatment for PVD?

The two most important treatments for PVD are aggressive modification of risk factors and a daily walking program. It is extremely important that the risk factors mentioned above be controlled to prevent these blockages from becoming worse over time. The most effective steps that patients can take to modify these risk factors are to stop cigarette smoking and lower their cholesterol, diabetes, and blood pressures to normal recommended levels.

Walking is very important to help maintain muscle tone, lower body weight, and develop better circulation to the feet. Patients should try and achieve a goal of walking 30 minutes a day, at least 5 days a week. There is one medication that has been approved by the FDA, called Pletal® , that can help improve blood flow to the feet. Pletal® has been shown to increase the distance patients can walk before they develop claudication. For mild claudication, it is a very effective medication. It does not by itself, however, "dissolve" the blockages that are in the arteries, and patients with moderate-to-severe claudication frequently require procedures to open up blocked arteries.

What types of procedures can be performed to open blocked arteries in the legs?

Similar to the heart, arteries in the legs can be opened

by using catheters with balloons and stents or by surgery to bypass the blocked vessel. Patients typically prefer balloons and stents because this is less invasive. This is called a ***percutaneous procedure***, in contrast to the surgical one that requires a ***bypass***. Percutaneous procedures significantly shorten recovery time with less discomfort, and the long-term outcome results are as good as or better than surgery. Therefore, the first-line approach to opening blocked blood vessels in the legs should be with a balloon or stent if the blockage is amenable to this kind of therapy. If the artery cannot be successfully opened percutaneously, then surgery is an alternative.

What risks are possible with angioplasty to the legs?

Although angioplasty and stents are preferred to surgery, these procedures are not without risks. Major complications can happen, although infrequently.

The following is a list of the most important serious complications:

♥ death (0.1%)

♥ major bleeding (2-3%)

♥ limb loss particularly in the patients with advanced lack of blood supply to the legs (1%)

♥ kidney failure (1-10%) especially in the patient with heart failure, preexisting kidney disease and diabetes

♥ early closure of the artery after as successful treatment that will require subsequent treatments

♥ damage to the blood vessels and nerves at the
puncture site (typically in the groin)
♥ to a lesser extent, infections, strokes and heart attacks

What risks are possible with surgery to the legs?

Surgery to the legs can carry all of the above risks in
addition to a longer recovery phase from generally bigger
wounds.

What is an Aneurysm?

An *aneurysm* is a "weakened" area of an artery that
is bulging out in the same way that a garden hose may
develop a bulge at a weak spot (*see Figure 1*). The danger
in aneurysms is if they become large enough, they can
spontaneously rupture. Aneurysms can occur throughout the
body but most commonly occur in the main aorta that runs
down through the chest and abdomen. If an aortic aneurysm
were to rupture, this could be a life-threatening event.
Therefore, aneurysms are typically repaired with surgery
or, more recently, with less invasive stent grafting, prior to
rupture.

Unfortunately, many times aneurysms do not have any
symptoms until they begin to rupture. If your doctor suspects
the presence of an aneurysm on examination, further testing
can be ordered to evaluate the presence of an aneurysm in
you. Screening for aortic aneurysms can be done using an
abdominal ultrasound or CT scan.

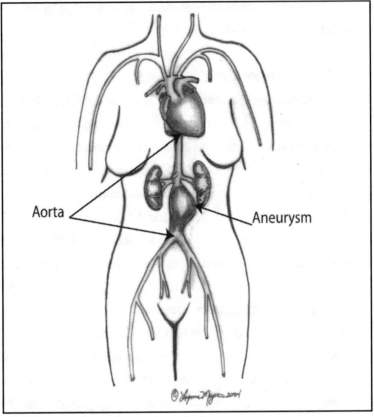

Figure 1. Aneurysm in the abdominal aorta.

Why do my legs swell?

Leg swelling, or *edema*, can be caused by a number of reasons. Some of these problems may be quite serious, while others are rather benign and cosmetic. Swelling in both legs may represent a heart or kidney problem, or a more benign problem is incompetent valves in the veins of the legs (varicose veins). Swelling in one leg may represent a blood clot in that leg or a blockage in the lymph nodes in the groin. It is also common for a leg to swell after veins have been removed for coronary artery bypass grafting. Any new swelling of one or both legs should be evaluated by your primary care physician.

What is Abdominal Angina?

Abdominal angina is pain in the abdomen resulting from blockages to the main arteries that supply the guts. It typically presents itself with pain in the abdomen after eating that cannot be explained by gastrointestinal pathology such as gallbladder disease or ulcers or inflammatory diseases. Blockages in those arteries called the celiac arteries or mesenteric arteries can lead to a reduction in the blood supply needed for digestion and transport of food to the body from the guts.

Patients typically experience predictable pain in the abdomen with food and weight loss. Cholesterol plaques cause a narrowing in these arteries similar to blockages in the neck, heart and legs. Treatment of these blockages can be done with either surgery or with angioplasty and stents. The diagnosis is best made by a CT angiogram or a conventional angiogram in the catheterization laboratory.

Generally, treatment of these blockages can lead to resolution of symptoms almost immediately after the procedure.

Summary: Ways we can reduce the risks or impact of Peripheral Vascular Disease (PVD)

♥ Quit smoking
♥ Walk at least 30 minutes 5 times per week
♥ Maintain an appropriate body weight
♥ Reduce blood pressure and cholesterol

♥ Aggressively manage your diabetes with the help of your doctor and dietitian

♥ Seek medical attention promptly if experiencing foot pain at night, along with discomfort in the calves when walking a short distance.

Chapter 5

Diseases of the Blood Vessels
of the Head and Neck

Eric J. Dippel, MD, FACC

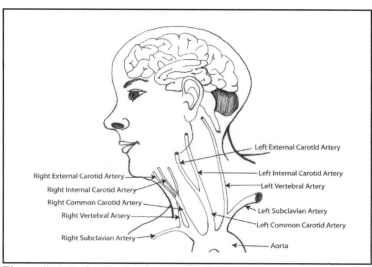

Figure 1. Arteries that lead to the brain.

What are the blood vessels that lead to the brain?

There are four major blood vessels that go to the brain:
two *carotid arteries* and two *vertebral arteries (see figure 1)*.
The two carotid arteries are in the front part of the neck; these
can actually be felt pulsating adjacent to your Adam's apple,
just below the angle of the jaw. The two vertebral arteries
go to the back of the brain and run in the bony portion of the
spine. All four arteries connect with each other in the brain.

What is Carotid Artery Disease (CAD)?

Carotid arteries, like the other arteries in the body, can become clogged with cholesterol over time. The risk factors that cause these blockages include: high cholesterol, cigarette smoking, diabetes, high blood pressure, and family history. When the carotid arteries become severely narrowed, this can lead to decreased blood flow to the brain, which can subsequently lead to a *stroke*.

What are the symptoms of Carotid Artery Disease?

Carotid artery disease is not associated with pain in the neck or headaches. When the carotid arteries become significantly narrowed, the blood can actually be heard "whooshing" through the blockage when a physician listens to the neck with a stethoscope. This noise is called a *bruit*. Some patients might experience chest pain and/or dizziness.

What are the risk factors for Carotid Artery Disease?

The risk factors for carotid artery disease are the same as for a stroke:

♥ Hypertension (high blood pressure)

♥ Diabetes

♥ A genetic tendency (family history)

♥ Prior stroke or TIA

♥ Lack of exercise

♥ Poor diet

♥ Obesity

♥ Possibly uncontrolled stress

How can a person prevent blockage in the carotid arteries?

The buildup of cholesterol, or *atherosclerosis*, in the carotid arteries occurs for the same reason cholesterol builds up in other arteries of the body. In fact, many patients that have coronary artery disease (CAD) or *peripheral vascular disease* (PVD) also have carotid disease. Aggressive modification of the risk factors that cause *atherosclerosis* will prevent the buildup of cholesterol in the arteries. This includes stopping smoking, lowering your cholesterol, controlling diabetes and high blood pressure, maintaining an ideal body weight, and getting regular exercise.

What kinds of tests can diagnose Carotid Artery Disease?

The simplest test is merely listening to the neck with a stethoscope for a bruit. Sometimes, however, bruits may be difficult to hear. A more accurate noninvasive test is a *carotid Doppler*, which is simply an *ultrasound* of the blood flow through the neck. *CT scanning* and *MR scanning* can also be helpful in providing three-dimensional images of the carotid and vertebral arteries. Finally, the "gold standard" is an *angiogram*, which is an invasive test where a catheter is inserted in the groin and threaded up to the carotid and vertebral arteries. Contrast dye is injected through the catheter and x-ray movie pictures are taken of the arteries in the neck.

When should a person have a procedure to open the neck arteries?

Whether or not carotid arteries should be treated with a procedure to open them up depends on several factors. One of the primary factors is whether the patient has had a prior symptom, such as a *stroke* or *TIA*, and the second major factor is the degree of *stenosis*, or narrowing in the artery. In combination, these findings have provided a framework for who should have a procedure to open the arteries versus who should simply continue on medical therapy to prevent further buildup of cholesterol.

How can blocked arteries in the neck be reopened?

Historically, the primary way to open up the carotid arteries is with surgery. This procedure has been performed for approximately 50 years and involves a surgeon cutting open the artery, scraping out the plaque, and sewing the artery back together. This procedure is known as a *carotid endarterectomy (CEA)*. Within the past few years, however, technology has evolved to the point where now the arteries can be opened up with a balloon and a *stent* via a catheter inserted through the groin under minimally invasive techniques. Recent data comparing carotid stenting versus surgery suggests that in certain high-risk groups of patients, stenting appears to be superior to surgery. Ongoing studies are being conducted to evaluate the carotid stenting procedure for lower-risk patients.

What is an Aneurysm?

An *aneurysm* is a weakened segment of an artery that is bulging out, similar to the way a garden hose will bulge out at a weak point. The problem with aneurysms is that they are prone to rupture, which will cause bleeding in the brain and a stroke. Unfortunately, however, most people do not know that they have an aneurysm in their brain until it ruptures, because they typically do not have any symptoms beforehand, other than possible non-specific headaches. Aneurysms are usually a genetic problem, so if there is a family history of aneurysms, it would be worthwhile to be screened for one *(see Figure 2)*.

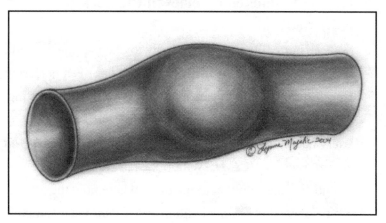

Figure 2. Aneurysm.

How Are Aneurysms in the brain treated?

The traditional way to treat aneurysms in the brain was by surgery to clip the aneurysm sac. However, with recent advances in cardiac procedures, it is now possible to thread a small catheter up the artery from the groin into the brain and place small coils inside the aneurysm. The advantages of using the catheters are that the skull does not have to be opened and the recovery time is significantly less.

Summing up . . . .

If you smoke, stop. Eat healthfully, maintain an appropriate body weight, get plenty of exercise. If you have high blood pressure, get it under control with a combination of weight loss, healthful eating, exercise and medication, as prescribed by your doctor. If you have a family history of aneurysms, get screened.

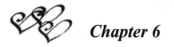 *Chapter 6*

Strokes:
How to Survive Them
and How to Prevent Them

Vickie S. Takes, RTR

Stroke is the third leading cause of death in the U.S. and the first leading cause of permanent disability in adults. **Stroke is preventable and treatable**, and the chances of having a severe disability can be reduced if people **recognize the symptoms** and **act quickly.**

What is a Stroke?

A *stroke* is a sudden death of brain cells due to a blood vessel rupture or a blood vessel blocked by a blood clot. Because of this rupture or blockage, the brain does not get the blood and oxygen it needs. When this happens, the brain cells in the affected area cannot work and die within minutes. The effects of a severe stroke are often permanent because brain cells are not replaced.

There are two major types of stroke: ischemic and hemorrhagic. *Ischemic stroke* is caused by blood clots or other particles. *Hemorrhagic stroke* is caused by bleeding. Bleeding strokes have a much higher death rate.

Ischemic stroke occurs more frequently than hemorrhagic stroke and accounts for approximately 70-80%

58

of all strokes. Ischemic stroke is a sudden reduction in blood flow to the brain. This occurs when a *blood clot (thrombus)* forms in an artery bringing blood to the brain. Blood clots form in arteries that are damaged by fatty cholesterol build-up, called *atherosclerosis*.

♥ *Cerebral thrombotic (blood clot) strokes* occur often at night or early morning. They are also usually preceded by a transient ischemic attack (TIA).

♥ *Transient ischemic attack (TIA)* is a short episode, less than 24 hours, of temporary impairment to the brain that is caused by a loss of blood supply. TIA's are often warnings of an impending stroke and must be immediately evaluated by a physician.

♥ A *moving clot (embolus)* or some other particle that forms away from the brain (usually in the heart) can also cause an ischemic stroke. The clot moves in the bloodstream until it becomes lodged in an artery leading to the brain, again blocking blood flow. *Atrial fibrillation (irregular heart beat)* is the most common cause of *embolization* or migration of a clot from the heart to the brain.

♥ The other 20% of strokes are caused by sudden excessive bleeding in the brain, called a *hemorrhage*.

There are two types of hemorrhage: subarachnoid and cerebral. *Subarachnoid hemorrhage* occurs when a blood vessel on the surface of the brain ruptures and bleeds into the space between the brain and the skull. *Cerebral hemorrhage* occurs when a blood vessel in the brain ruptures and bleeds into the surrounding tissue. The amount of bleeding determines the severity of the stroke. The chance of dying is higher with a hemorrhagic stroke versus an ischemic stroke due to increased pressure on the brain, but those people who survive tend to recover much more than people that have had a stroke caused by a clot.

What are the risk factors of having a stroke?

Knowing your risk factors may help you to prevent a stroke.

Risk Factors You Can Change

♥ **Smoking** – Stop smoking . . . now . . . for good!

♥ **Hypertension** *(High Blood Pressure)* – Get your blood pressure checked and take measures to lower it if it's too high. Anything higher than 130/85 needs to be lowered. A regimen of appropriate diet, exercise and medication can help lower your blood pressure.

♥ **High Cholesterol Levels** – There are two types of cholesterol, "good" and "bad." The good cholesterol (or HDL) transports cholesterol from the blood vessels to the liver whereas the bad cholesterol (LDL) sends cholesterol from the liver into the blood vessel. Know what your cholesterol levels (including HDL and LDL) are and what they mean. Ask your doctor to check them if you do not know. Continue to have them checked regularly. If you are prescribed cholesterol medicine, take it as directed. Choose foods that will lower your "bad" cholesterol and increase your "good" cholesterol.

♥ **Uncontrolled Diabetes** – Uncontrolled diabetes can accelerate atherosclerosis (blockage of the arteries).

Seek medical attention and engage in the appropriate balance of diet, exercise and medication to control your blood sugar.

♥ **Lack of Exercise** – Increase your activity. Even a short walk every day will increase your well-being and may lead to a more active life.

♥ **Poor Diet** – Learn about good and bad fats and how to improve your diet to a healthy one that will increase your well-being and enjoyment of life.

♥ **Uncontrolled Stress** – Stress levels can be changed or better managed if you educate yourself on what causes your stress and learn stress-reduction techniques.

Risk Factors You Can't Change

♥ **Genetics** – You can't change who your parents are and what they pass on to you, so if your parents have had a stroke, it might increase your risk of having a stroke. You can educate yourself on how to maximize your health situation and change the risk factors that you can.

♥ **Age** – The older we are, the higher the chance of a stroke occurring.

♥ **Gender** – Men develop symptomatic disease at an earlier age, but women are also at risk.

What are the warning signs of a stroke?

The American Stroke Association wants you to learn the warning signs of a stroke. If you notice one or more of these signs, **DON'T WAIT. CALL 9-1-1 and get to the hospital immediately!**

Warning signs of a stroke include:

♥ Sudden numbness or weakness of the face, arm or leg, especially on one side of the body

♥Sudden confusion, trouble speaking or understanding

♥ Sudden visual problems, double vision or sudden loss of vision

♥ Sudden trouble walking, dizziness, loss of balance or coordination

♥ Sudden, severe headache with no known cause

What should I do if I suspect a stroke?

♥ Not all the warning signs occur in every stroke. Don't ignore signs of stroke, even if they go away!

♥ Check the time. When did the first warning sign or symptom start? You'll be asked this important question later.

♥ If you have one or more stroke symptoms that last more than a few minutes, don't delay! **Immediately call 9-1-1** or the emergency medical service number so an ambulance can quickly respond.

♥ If you're with someone who may be having stroke symptoms, **call 9-1-1**. Expect the person to protest; denial is common. ***Don't take "No" for an answer. Insist on taking action!***

How do I know if I have had a stroke?

Anyone who may be having a stroke should go to an emergency center immediately. The doctors will get a medical history from you. If you or the person who is experiencing symptoms is unable to give a history, then

others who know the patient will be asked to assist. A
neurologist – a doctor specializing in the nervous system and
brain disorders – will be called to assist in the diagnosis and
management of the stroke patient.

CT Scan (Computerized Tomography) will be ordered.
A CT scan – a special x-ray of the brain – will confirm the
stroke and distinguish between ischemic and hemorrhagic
stroke.

MRI Scan (Magnetic Resonance Imaging) is another
method of viewing the brain. Although the MRI scan is able
be get much more detailed pictures of the brain, the CT scan
is the first procedure performed.

Conventional Angiogram is another test that can be
performed to view the blood vessels, carotid arteries and the
brain.

Carotid Ultrasound is a non-invasive test that uses
sound waves to detect narrowing and a slowing or reduction
in blood flow through the carotid arteries.

Echocardiogram is a test to evaluate the function of
the heart. This test is done on stroke patients, in search of the
source of an embolism.

Electrocardiogram (EKG or ECG) is a test that can be
done to check your heart rhythm. An irregular heartbeat can
be a source of an embolism that can cause a stroke.

Treatment options for stroke

TPA: TPA (tissue plasminogen activator) is a new
medication developed during the last few years for immediate
treatment of stroke. TPA is a clot-buster medication that if
given within the **first three hours** of the onset of symptoms

through an I.V. has been shown to improve the patient's long-term outcome from a stroke. The three-hour time frame is critical and, again, is why you need to seek help immediately.

Aspirin and Heparin: Medications such as aspirin and heparin, which are used to thin the blood, sometimes are used to treat patients in hopes of improving the patient's recovery from a stroke. It is not clear if this improves the stroke or if it helps to prevent more strokes. If a patient is unable to take aspirin, new antiplatelet medications such as clopidogrel (Plavix) and ticlopidine (Ticlid) are available.

Which medical procedures might prevent a stroke?

Carotid Endarterectomy: an operation for Carotid Artery Disease, to clean out the plaque causing the narrowing or ulceration of the carotid artery.

Carotid Stenting: the most recent treatment for carotid artery disease. A ***stent (metal tube)*** is inserted into the carotid artery to open the narrowing or ulceration and stabilize the carotid artery. These procedures are explained in more detail in Chapter 5.

How does someone recover from a stroke?

After a stroke, the affected area of the brain dies and probably will not recover its function. When a patient has stabilized after a stroke, the focus begins on rehabilitation. The goal is to maximize the patient's recovery to be able to return to his or her normal daily activities. Therapies available include ***speech therapy***, to help the patient to learn to eat and speak again; *occupational therapy*, to relearn the use of your arms and hands; and *physical therapy*, to regain strength and possibly regain the ability to walk.

Even though the goal is to help the person regain the ability to engage in former daily activities, this is usually not realistic. The patient and family members will also be educated on how to adjust to these changes and to live as full a life as possible.

Chapter 7

Valvular Heart Disease

Girish R. Bhatt, MD, FACC, FACP

What are heart valves?

The heart is a machine, a pump, and like any other pump, for the heart to work efficiently, it needs valves. *Heart valves* are basically designed to regulate the amount, direction and appropriate blood flow so that body organs receive proportionate blood, a vehicle to supply nutrients and oxygen to the body. Despite the fact that heart valves are very delicate structures, nature has designed them in such a way that ordinarily they function well throughout human life. However, the complexity of their structure makes them vulnerable to many damaging processes, such as degeneration, infection, inflammation or congenital deformities.

Where are the heart valves located?

Basically, there are four heart valves: two in the left side and two in the right side of the heart cavity. The heart valve that is located between the left upper heart chamber and the left lower heart chamber is termed the *mitral valve.* Medically, the left upper chamber is called the *left atrium*, and the left lower chamber is called the *left ventricle*. The heart valve that is located between the main left chamber (left ventricle) and the main body artery (***aorta***) is called the ***aortic valve***. The heart valve located between the right upper chamber (right atrium) and the right lower chamber (right ventricle) is called the ***tricuspid valve***. The heart valve located between the right lower chamber (right ventricle) and ***pulmonary artery*** (main lung artery) is called the ***pulmonary valve*** *(see figure 1).*

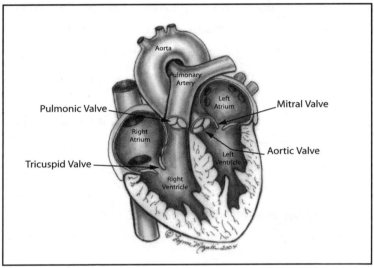

Figure 1. Valves of the heart.

How do heart valves function?

The basic function of the heart valves is to allow passage of blood to the heart chambers and from the heart chamber to the body and lungs. Heart valves operate through pressure changes between two adjacent chambers and vessels. For example, when the left lower chamber (left ventricle) contracts, pressure within the cavity increases, which opens the aortic valve.

On the other hand, when the left ventricle relaxes, pressure within its cavity falls below that of the aorta (*distal vessel*), and that closes the aortic valve. Similar pressure changes occur across other valves which open and close the valves appropriately. Valve structure integrity is vital to the opening and closing of the heart valves.

How does valvular heart disease occur?

Two principal ways in which valve dysfunction can occur are known as *stenosis* (narrowing of the heart valve) and *regurgitation* (leakage of the heart valve). For example, *aortic stenosis* means that the aortic valve is narrow; therefore, it will not allow the appropriate amount of blood to go from the left ventricle to the aorta. It will also imply that the left ventricle will have to work much harder (and, hence, spend much more energy) to let the blood go through the aortic valve. *Aortic regurgitation* means that blood is leaking backward from the aorta to the left ventricle. The same terminology is applied for the mitral valve, tricuspid valve and pulmonary valves.

There are various ways through which valvular dysfunction can occur:

1. Congenital Heart Disease: Inborn error in the structure and function of the heart valve. This is generally secondary to developmental malfunction and gets detected at a very early age. Advances in pediatric cardiology have made prognosis of these diseases significantly better.

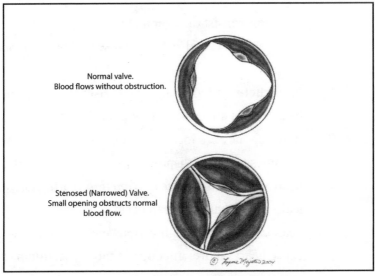

Normal valve.
Blood flows without obstruction.

Stenosed (Narrowed) Valve.
Small opening obstructs normal
blood flow.

Normal Aortic Valve (top) and diseased Aortic Valve (bottom).

2. Infection: The first notable cause is *rheumatic fever*. A very common disease of the last century and the earlier part of the 20th century, rheumatic fever has vanished quickly through our ability to eradicate infection. However, this still remains a real health problem, primarily in underdeveloped countries. In adult life, infections such as those caused by bacteria can result in valvular heart dysfunction; medically, this is known as *bacterial endocarditis*. However, it is very uncommon for a normal heart valve to get infected. Generally, secondary heart valve infections occur in patients who have been suffering from congenital or rheumatic heart diseases. Rheumatic fever is caused by a bacterial infection known as *streptococcus*. Primary manifestations of this infection consist of fever and multiple joint pains. This bacteria can also cause a disease known as *scarlet fever*.

3. Structural Valvular Heart Disease: Mechanically, heart valves are designed for appropriate cavity size in which they are located. If for any reason a cavity becomes enlarged disproportionate to the size of the heart valve, *heart valve dysfunction* (particularly leakage) of that valve can occur. Enlargement of the heart can occur through various mechanisms that cause heart failure, infection in the myocardium (heart muscle) and sudden acute processes, such as heart attacks.

4. Various Other Mechanisms: Fibrosis and calcium deposits (aging process) and various other rare processes, such as myxomatous degradation (abnormal substance deposition in heart valve) or certain weight-loss drugs, also can cause valvular dysfunction.

How does valvular heart disease affect the human body?

The ultimate adverse outcome of valvular heart disease is heart failure. However, it may take a long time (sometimes years) before overt manifestations of heart failure occur after onset of valvular heart disease.

What are the symptoms of heart failure?

The main symptoms of heart failure are *fatigue* (tiredness), *dyspnea* (shortness of breath) and edema (swelling of the feet). The patient may experience lack of vigor and vitality and/or may simply feel "I'm not feeling as well as before."

Heart failure can worsen or can be worsened by other co-existent conditions, such as ***anemia*** (low blood count) and ***pregnancy***.

How is valvular heart disease diagnosed?

There are various ways by which your doctor can diagnose heart disease.

1. **Physical Examination:** The most common manifestation of valvular heart disease is **heart murmur**, a noise that occurs when the blood passes through a particular valve. Ordinarily, passage of the blood through a heart valve is so smooth that a physician cannot detect any murmur when he listens to the chest of a patient through the stethoscope. It should be noted that not all heart murmurs necessarily represent valvular heart disease. Approximately 10% to 20% of heart murmurs are innocent and are termed ***benign heart murmurs***. Many times, these heart murmurs disappear as age advances, and even if they may persist, they may not cause any heart problem. Occasionally, heart murmurs can also occur in the absence of valvular heart disease, such as pregnancy, anemia or ***thyrotoxicosis*** (excess thyroid hormone production).

2. **Echocardiogram:** ***Echocardiogram (heart ultrasound)*** has revolutionized diagnosis of valvular heart disease. This very simple and mostly non-invasive test does not only accurately detect the valvular heart

disease but also can define its severity, prognosis and also direct appropriate management.

An additional recently added feature to sonographic examination of the heart is called ***Doppler study***. This method works through pressure principles of physics and adds to the accuracy of sonographic evaluation. A color component added to Doppler studies can actually visualize the blood flow through various heart valves. Serial echocardiographic evaluations (semi-annually or annually) can help judge progress of the disease and/or can help determine optimal time for intervention. This painless, non-invasive procedure also allows the cardiologist to determine heart pump function.

Progress in science of ***echocardiography*** is continuous, and even 3-dimensional echocardiography is not far from reality. Trained technologists known as cardiac sonographers perform the procedures and the cardiologist interprets them. The procedure itself lasts for 30-45 minutes and has become widely available throughout the United States.

3. Cardiac Catheterization: This is an invasive procedure performed through introduction of a catheter via a peripheral vein and/or artery (generally through the groin, known as *femoral vein* and *femoral artery*). Although diagnostic in nature, these procedures are generally performed prior to intervention (e.g., prior to cardiac valve surgery). Although invasive, these procedures are generally considered safe, and the complication rate is below 0.5% in institutions where these procedures are performed in adequate numbers. The procedure is similar to coronary angiogram, with the difference that the catheters enter the heart chambers in cardiac catheterization. Valvular diseases are detected through direct inspection (*visualization*) and pressure measurements. Cardiac catheterization is, at least at the present time, considered ultimate, the "gold standard."

What happens once heart valve disease is detected?

Treatment of heart valve disease depends upon the patient's clinical status (symptoms and signs), severity of valvular heart disease and expected outcome after its treatment. Most often, valvular heart diseases require surgery for their correction. These procedures are known as **heart valve replacements**.

Technology has, however, advanced, and in some instances, particularly in mitral and tricuspid valves, repair valvular surgery can also be undertaken. As a matter of fact, these repair procedures are gaining more acceptance because they preserve the natural integrity of the heart valves. Even though heart valve replacement requires open-heart surgery, the morbidity/mortality rate (death rate) remains acceptable and varies between 2% to 10%, depending upon the patient's condition and co-existent problems.

What are the types of heart valves?

Heart valves are of two types. The first category is *mechanical heart valves*. These are also known as "metal" heart valves. The second category is ***bioprosthetic ("tissue") heart valves***. Commonly, these are also referred to as "pig valves." A cardiovascular surgeon would determine what kind of heart valve one should get. Although both categories of these heart valves have performed very well throughout the years, there are some differences between these categories. The foremost difference is the lifetime of the heart valve. Metal heart valves generally last longer compared to tissue heart valves. On the other hand, mechanical (metal) heart valves require ***anticoagulation*** (thinning of the blood), generally through the use of the drug Warfarin (Coumadin).

Many factors enter into consideration while determining the type of heart valve to be used. For example, if valvular heart surgery is chosen in the older age group and when use of Coumadin is thought to be associated with high risks, bioprosthetic (tissue) valves are chosen. The converse may be true for younger individuals.

What can someone expect after valvular heart surgery?

The most important factor in determining the outcome of valvular heart surgery is ***optimal timing***. Therefore, it is of paramount importance that the patient follow up with his/her cardiologist in a very regular fashion once heart valve disease is detected. The patient's functional status, physical examination, serial echocardiographic evaluation, cardiac catheterization and other factors may determine the need for surgery. One such other factor can be pregnancy. Because pregnancy imposes additional stress on circulation, physicians may decide to undertake valvular heart surgery prior to pregnancy and delivery.

One may expect quite a good prognosis after heart valve surgery. Improvements would include not only better functional status (that is, the ability to perform ordinary activities) but also overall survival prognosis.

Because valvular heart diseases take months and years for their full adverse effects, it may take some time (usually more than 6 months or a year) before a patient would fully recognize the benefit of surgery. Periodic checkups are a necessity, even after successful surgery.

What is prophylactic antibiotic?

In medical terms, administering antibiotics to prevent infection on the heart valves is known as ***prophylaxis for subacute bacterial endocarditis (SBE).*** The presence of valvular heart disease (even after surgery) mandates that the patient receives appropriate antibiotic(s) prior to undergoing certain procedures (such as dental procedures or other surgeries) or prior to anticipated infections. The American Heart Association has published appropriate guidelines for this purpose. However, it is of utmost importance that the patient keep the dentist or other physician(s) informed of the nature of his/her heart valve disease.

Heart valve diseases are generally chronic and progressive in nature. However, they may also occur acutely. Notable examples are after heart attack or after acute infections. Generally, surgery is needed for severe valvular heart diseases for optimal outcome. However, medical therapy is also carried out most often as adjunct therapy. It

75

should not be forgotten that once it occurs, valvular heart disease is a lifelong process. Therefore, it is vital that it will be followed by an appropriate physician (generally a cardiologist) throughout its course.

Significant progress has been made in this category of heart diseases during the last half century, and progress continues. Once thought relentless and progressive, these diseases can be prevented and appropriately cared for by the progress that the science of Cardiology has fulfilled through many last decades.

 *Chapter 8*

Heart Rhythms: How to Recognize Them and Treat Them

Mark W. Kovach, MD, FACC

What is atrial fibrillation?

The normal heart beats approximately 60 to 100 times a minute. However, many heart patients experience problems when the heart rhythm is disrupted and their heart beats either too quickly or too slowly.

Atrial fibrillation is one the most common heart rhythm problems that physicians treat. Atrial fibrillation is a rapid irregular electrical activity of the upper chambers of the heart, called the *atria*. When it occurs intermittently in some patients, this is called *paroxysmal atrial fibrillation*. In other patients, the atrial fibrillation can be persistent for many months and is called *chronic atrial fibrillation*.

Some patients are very symptomatic when their heart rhythm goes into atrial fibrillation, while others have little or no symptoms at all. Symptoms can range from mild palpitations to shortness of breath, heart racing, lightheadedness or passing-out spells. The treatment that doctors recommend depends, in part, on how symptomatic the atrial fibrillation is in a particular patient.

What are the causes of atrial fibrillation?

There is no one specific cause of atrial fibrillation, but it is frequently seen in association with other medical problems. It is often associated with high blood pressure and becomes increasingly more common as people age. In fact, in people over the age of 80, approximately 1 in 10 have this heart rhythm problem. Occasionally atrial fibrillation can occur in young people without any associated medical problems. In these people we call their atrial fibrillation "**lone atrial fibrillation.**"

Atrial fibrillation can also occur because of elevated thyroid gland function. A blood test to check the level of thyroid hormones in patients with atrial fibrillation should be routinely done. In addition, patients with weak heart muscle, problems with blockages in the coronaries and valves of the heart, or viral infection to the heart can have atrial fibrillation. In hospitalized patients, clots migrating to the lungs (typically from the veins of the lower legs), called *pulmonary emboli*, can also cause atrial fibrillation.

The typical testing to uncover the cause of atrial fibrillation includes an ultrasound to the heart *(echocardiogram)*, thyroid function tests and other blood tests, stress test to rule out blockages in the coronaries, and occasionally a scan on the lung to rule out a clot, if clinically suspected.

What are the two main types of treatment for atrial fibrillation?

There are two main types of treatment for atrial fibrillation: *rate control* and *rhythm control*.

What is rate control of atrial fibrillation?

With rate control, the simplest form of treatment, the heart is allowed to continue its paroxysmal or chronic atrial fibrillation without trying to force a heart rhythm back into regular rhythm. The speed by which the heart beats, however, is controlled. Certain types of medications are often used to make sure if the heart goes rapidly when it is out of rhythm, that the rate is slowed down to within the normal range. The goal of this treatment is to make sure that the heart does not beat too quickly or too slowly. Occasionally, the medications used to prevent the heart from going too fast will at times cause the heart rate to go too slowly. When this happens, doctors may recommend treatment with a pacemaker to prevent the slow heart rates. While pacemakers do not prevent atrial fibrillation in general, they are very good at preventing slow heart rhythms, which can cause dizziness or fainting spells.

In addition, people who have long episodes or persistent atrial fibrillation are at risk for blood clots and strokes, so doctors frequently recommend "blood thinner" medications. The most commonly prescribed medication for preventing blood clots and strokes in patients with atrial fibrillation is a medication called Coumadin. While this medication is reasonably safe in most patients, as long as it is regulated closely, in some patients it can be quite difficult to regulate and can cause bleeding problems if the blood becomes "too thin." Coumadin needs to be closely regulated by your physician or special clinics called anticoagulation/coumadin clinics.

Without adequate rate control, the fast heartbeats can lead to weakening of the heart muscle and can result in a condition of fluid buildup known as *congestive heart failure*. Controlling the heart rate can reverse this condition if caused primarily by the atrial fibrillation.

What is rhythm control of atrial fibrillation?

The other main treatment for atrial fibrillation is *rhythm control*. With rhythm control, the goal is to get the heart back into regular rhythm and to keep it in rhythm. This usually requires stronger heart medicines called *anti-arrhythmics*. These medications can have serious side effects in some patients and have to be followed closely by a physician.

Sometimes it is necessary to shock the heart back into rhythm using a treatment called *cardioversion*, during which a synchronized electrical shock is delivered to the chest of a patient who is closely monitored and sedated. The success rate for keeping the heart in rhythm is not 100% and it is common for patients to have recurrences of their atrial fibrillation, despite receiving cardioversions and taking strong anti-arrhythmic medications. Frequently, doctors will still place these patients on blood thinners such as Coumadin.

What are ventricular tachycardia and ventricular fibrillation?

Ventricular tachycardia and *ventricular fibrillation* are abnormal fast heart rhythms which arise from the bottom part of the heart, called the *ventricles*.

In *ventricular tachycardia*, the heart can beat at 200-300 beats per minute. These fast heartbeats do not allow adequate filling of the blood inside the heart chambers leading to a drop in blood pressure and frequently loss of consciousness. In *ventricular fibrillation*, the heart rhythm is very fast and disorganized. During this rhythm, no blood can be ejected out of the ventricles and death is imminent if the ventricular fibrillation is not immediately corrected.

Ventricular tachycardia most frequently occurs in people who have significant heart disease. Less often, ventricular tachycardia can occur in people who have no significant heart disease, and in these patients, the rhythms are benign. However, when ventricular tachycardia and ventricular fibrillation occur in people who have heart disease, these rhythms can be life-threatening. Quite often, ventricular tachycardia can cause shortness of breath, lightheadedness, passing-out spells, and can in some instances lead to cardiac arrest. Ventricular fibrillation and and fibrillation are the most common cause of death after a heart attack.

What is a pacemaker?

When the heartbeats are abnormally slow, a *pacemaker* might become necessary. A pacemaker is a special medical device which delivers a minimum number of electrical impulses to the heart per minute *(see Figure 1)*. These electrical impulses stimulate the muscle of the heart to beat. A pacemaker is made of an electrical generator (that generates the electrical impulse) placed under the skin and is attached to a wire that sets in the heart and conducts the electricity from the generator to the heart muscle.

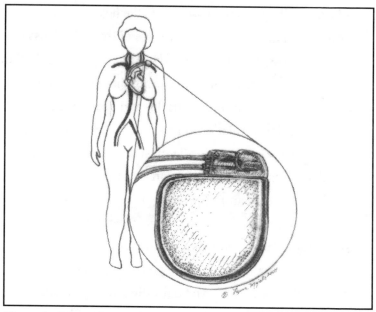

Figure 1. Pacemaker, and common location of implant.

Most pacemakers work on what is called a "***demand mode.***" This means that pacemakers only "kick in" or pace the heart when the heart rate tries to slow down. Some pacemakers can only pace the bottom of the heart (the ventricle), while others can pace in both the top of the heart (the atria), as well as the ventricle. More recently, special pacemakers have been developed which can make the heart beat more efficiently in certain patients who suffer from weakening of the heart muscle called congestive heart failure.

It is important to remember that in most people, the pacemaker's primary job is to prevent slow heart rhythms.

What is a defibrillator?

A *defibrillator* is a device that is slightly larger than a pacemaker, inserted under the skin and connected to the heart by a wire. Defibrillators can sense serious fast heart rhythms such as ventricular fibrillation or ventricular tachycardia and treat them by delivering an electrical shock to the heart. This electrical shock aborts those abnormal heart rhythms and allows the heart to restore its normal beating.

New defibrillators are sophisticated and capable of also pacing the heart if it slows down. Current defibrillators also are pacemakers. Defibrillators are very efficient and successful in treating fast as well as slow heart rhythms. The downside of defibrillator treatment is the occasional need for a shock to reset the heart to regular rhythm. These shocks, although uncomfortable, can be life-saving in patients who have these types of serious heart rhythm problems. Frequently an antiarrythmic medication is also prescribed for patients who have these types of serious heart rhythm problems, to prevent the heart from getting out of rhythm in the first place and minimize the shocks delivered by a defibrillator.

It is important to remember that defibrillators do not prevent the heart from going into these bad rhythms, but instead they correct irregular rhythms when they occur.

Often defibrillators are placed in patients who are thought by their physicians to be at high risk for having a ventricular rhythm in the future. Since these rhythms are dangerous and can lead to cardiac arrest and death, it is best to make sure that people who are at high risk have a defibrillator placed before one of these events can happen.

What is supraventricular tachycardia?

Supraventricular tachycardia, or SVT, is a type of fast heart rhythm which originates from the top part of the heart (atria) in some people. These episodes of heart racing can occur suddenly and last for several minutes to several hours, depending on the individual. The symptoms associated with this type of fast heart rhythm can range from mild palpitations to shortness of breath to chest pain, lightheadedness, or passing-out spells. In most patients, SVT is a benign condition.

In most cases of heart racing due to SVT, the episodes stop spontaneously after several minutes. Occasionally, these episodes can persist for longer periods of time and require a trip to the emergency room. These episodes can usually be terminated quite easily with certain types of medications that are given in the emergency room.

The long-term treatment for patients with SVT involves the use of either medications to try to suppress the fast heart rhythms or a special catheter procedure to try to get rid of the problem more definitively and permanently. *Electrophysiologists* are doctors who specialize in treating heart rhythm problems. Patients with frequent symptoms of SVT are often referred to electrophysiologists to be

84

evaluated whether they may benefit from a *catheter ablation* procedure. During a catheter ablation procedure, the origin of the abnormal heart rhythm is located and eliminated by an energy current called *radiofrequency current* delivered from the tip of a catheter placed in the heart chamber. This procedure is done under light sedation in the cardiac catheterization laboratory. If a successful catheter ablation is completed, it can eliminate the cause of SVT and can get rid of this type of heart racing altogether.

Can loss of consciousness be caused by abnormal heart rhythm?

Loss of consciousness can be caused by multiple reasons, including the heart, the brain or the nervous system that control the tone of the blood vessels. The heart can cause fainting spells if it goes too fast or too slowly. This can happen from any of the type of rhythm problems described in this chapter. Patients also can have severe narrowing in one of the heart valves, which can also cause a fainting spell, particularly with exertion. Identifying the cause of fainting or near-fainting spells can be very difficult and might require multiple testing. This can include tests to the heart such as an *ultrasound (or echocardiogram)*, an outpatient rhythm monitoring device, a stress test, an ultrasound to the carotid arteries (arteries that supply the brain) and a CT scan of the brain. Another test that is frequently done is called a *tilt table test*. A patient is typically placed on a table, strapped and tilted 80 degrees. The physician monitors the heart rhythm and blood pressure for about 20 minutes while the patient is tilted and occasionally administers medications to determine if the fainting spells reoccur. Usually, if this happens, the spell is probably related to an imbalance in the control of the tone of the blood vessels by the nervous system.

In about 20% of patients, the cause of the fainting spells remains unknown despite all the testing. Usually in about 6-7% of these patients, the fainting spell can recur.

What is a Holter monitor?

A **Holter monitor** is a device that a patient takes home for 24-48 hours and is attached to the chest by several wires that monitor the heart rhythm. All heartbeats during these hours are recorded on a tape. If a patient experiences a symptom, he or she notes the time and type of symptom on a diary and marks the event on the monitor. The physician reviews all the recorded heart rhythm and correlates it with the recorded event and symptoms on the diary. This helps determine whether the symptom is related to a rhythm problem. This test is reserved to those patients in whom symptoms occur frequently.

What is an event care monitor?

An **event care monitor** is essentially the same as a Holter monitor with the exception that it records the heart rhythm on demand as requested by the patient. A patient who experiences a symptom activates the device, which records the rhythm. This is then transmitted over a phone to a central station that analyzes the rhythm and informs the doctor of the results. A patient can keep the event monitor for a month. This test is reserved to those who have infrequent symptoms.

What should patients do if they experience palpitations in the chest?

A physician should evaluate palpitations, particularly if accompanied by chest pain, shortness of breath, dizzy spells or preceding fainting spells. **Patients who experience these symptoms should not drive themselves to the emergency room but should call 9-1-1.** Many palpitations are benign, but some are serious and could indicate an underlying cardiac disease such as a heart muscle or valves problem, or blockages in the coronaries. Palpitations, particularly those lasting for a beat or two, or a couple of seconds, are likely to be benign skipped beats if not accompanied by any other symptoms. Caffeinated beverages including coffee, tea and chocolate, or stress or deconditioning can precipitate these benign skipped beats. The determination whether skipped beats are benign or not is done after a careful and detailed evaluation by the physician. Patients should not try to self-diagnose or ignore these symptoms.

 *Chapter 9*

Congestive Heart Failure

Peter J. Sharis, MD

What is congestive heart failure?

If you have *congestive heart failure,* it means your heart does not work as well as it should, leading to high pressure inside the chambers of the heart. This can be the result of weak and/or stiff heart muscle. Symptoms of congestive heart failure include shortness of breath with activity, problems breathing when lying down, waking up at night short of breath or coughing, going to the bathroom many times at night, swollen feet or ankles, and general weakness or fatigue.

What causes congestive heart failure?

Congestive heart failure typically occurs when another problem makes the heart muscle weak. *Coronary artery disease*, which is due to cholesterol buildup (*atherosclerosis*) in the heart's own blood vessels, is a common cause of congestive heart failure. This buildup can lead to severe narrowings which reduce blood flow to the heart and make it pump weakly. When cholesterol plaque(s) crack or rupture, the resulting turbulent blood flow can lead to clot formation and near complete or complete occlusion of the blood vessel, which results in a *heart attack*. A heart attack results in permanent scarring or damage to the heart and thus decreases overall heart function, making congestive heart failure more likely to occur.

Another condition that contributes to congestive heart failure is **high blood pressure**. Individuals with high blood pressure often have a thick, muscular left ventricle, which is the main pumping chamber of the heart. When the muscle gets too thick, it starts to fail to relax adequately between heartbeats (during diastole). This can lead to congestive heart failure from **diastolic dysfunction**. About one-third of congestive heart failure cases have a diastolic dysfunction component.

Problems with the heart's valves can also lead to congestive heart failure. For example, if the **aortic valve**, which regulates blood flow from the left ventricle into the aorta, becomes severely narrowed, then the left ventricle has to pump harder to squeeze the same amount of blood through a smaller hole *(see Figure 1)*. Eventually

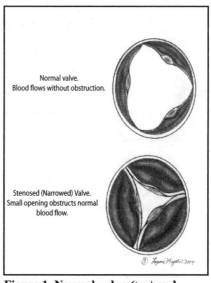

Figure 1. Normal valve *(top)* and narrow, diseased valve *(bottom)*.

the ventricle can become overwhelmed with this increasing load and beginning to fail, which leads to congestive heart failure. Other valve disorders in which a valve does not close properly – resulting in a *"leaky" valve*, where large amounts of blood essentially go backwards during portions of the cardiac cycle – can also lead to congestive heart failure.

Finally, damage to heart muscle from causes other than artery or blood flow problems is known as *cardiomyopathy* and can cause congestive heart failure. Cardiomyopathy can result from infections (*myocarditis*), alcohol abuse, diabetes, high blood pressure, muscle degeneration, and the toxic effects of certain drugs (e.g., cancer drugs and cocaine).

What signs are present on physical examination that indicates congestive heart failure?

If the heart muscle is damaged and weak this can often be discovered when the doctor feels for or palpates the area of the chest overlying the heart. When the physician listens to or *auscultates* the heart, murmurs, extra heart sounds, or arrhythmias may be present which indicate a particular underlying cause of congestive heart failure. Auscultation of the lungs may reveal lots of "crackles" due to the presence of fluid in the lungs, which is a common finding in acute congestive heart failure. Swelling (edema) may be present in the ankles and feet, or in severe cases, extending into the thighs and belly region.

Which types of noninvasive tests can be performed to help diagnose the cause of congestive heart failure?

A *chest x-ray* can provide information about the heart's shape and size. Abnormalities can suggest underlying weak heart function or the presence of significant valvular abnormalities. An *electrocardiogram (EKG)* shows the pattern of the heartbeat and also reveals data about the size of the heart chambers and whether there has been a prior heart attack. An *ultrasound of the heart* (called an *echocardiogram*) can provide detailed information about the size, structure, and movement of the heart muscle and valves. There are two types of *stress tests* that can be performed to determine the heart's response to exercise and can help detect narrowed and/or clogged heart vessels: *exercise-based* and *pharmacologic*. Pharmacologic tests are employed in people who cannot exercise easily on a treadmill; these tests utilize medications such as adenosine and dobutamine that stress the heart. *Nuclear scans* are often done in conjunction with stress tests; these pictures can help localize areas of the heart which have abnormal blood flow.

What information can cardiac catheterization provide about the cause and prognosis of congestive heart failure?

Cardiac catheterization is often performed to determine the problem(s) that led to the development of congestive heart failure. The procedure is done under local anesthesia with a large sheath being placed in the groin or arm area. Catheters are then guided up into the heart using x-ray guidance. Pressures can be measured within the heart's main pumping chamber and the squeezing power of the heart can be evaluated. A special kind of x-ray, called an *angiogram*, is then taken of the heart's arteries by injecting contrast dye directly into the main vessels that supply the heart. The angiogram pictures can reveal any clogged arteries or narrowings which can often be the primary cause of congestive heart failure.

Which treatment measures are available to treat congestive heart failure?

A typical treatment plan consists of multiple measures including some or all of the following:

♥ Medications to help remove fluid and make the heart work better

♥Dietary modifications such as reducing salt and cholesterol intake

♥ Lifestyle changes such as smoking cessation

♥ Exercise regimen

Which types of medications provide the most benefit in patients with congestive heart failure?

Vasodilators help to relax and dilate blood vessels so that blood flows more easily. This lowers blood pressure and allows the heart to pump more blood without doing more work. The most effective type of vasodilators are *ACE inhibitors*, which have been shown to reduce deaths in congestive heart failure due to weak heart function (systolic dysfunction). Other types of vasodilators include nitrates and hydralazine.

Diuretics work by removing the excess fluid from the body that often accumulates in those with congestive heart failure. Fluid removal reduces the workload of the heart since it has less fluid to circulate around the body. Since some diuretics deplete potassium levels, potassium supplements may be required in conjunction with diuretic therapy. Spironolactone and eplerenone are potassium-sparing diuretics which have recently been shown to have a significant benefit in congestive heart failure due to systolic dysfunction.

Beta blockers slow the heart rate and lower the blood pressure, which reduces the workload on the heart. Beta blockers appear to improve the pumping action of the heart over long periods of time and also are beneficial in those with congestive heart failure due to diastolic dysfunction, since a slower heart rate allows a stiff left ventricle to relax more.

Digoxin helps the heart pump more vigorously, resulting in more blood being pumped per heartbeat. Digoxin also helps to regulate a heartbeat that is too fast or irregular (e.g., atrial fibrillation). While long-term digoxin therapy has not been shown to reduce death, it does reduce the incidence of hospitalization in those with severe congestive heart failure.

Anticoagulants thin the blood and help to reduce the incidence of blood clots. Individuals who have atrial fibrillation, who have had valve surgery, or who have very weak hearts are prone to developing clots. Anticoagulants help to reduce the complications associated with clot formation, especially stroke.

Antiarrhythmics are utilized to help control irregular or rapid heart rates. Examples include amiodarone, beta-blockers, calcium channel blockers, and digoxin.

Which medications are used when patients require hospital admission due to congestive heart failure?

Intravenous medications are typically utilized when patients are sick enough to require admission for heart failure treatment. *Diuretics* are commonly used to aggressively remove excess fluid from the lungs and rest of the body. Potent intravenous medications called *inotropes* (examples: dopamine, dobutamine, milrinone) that help improve the heart squeeze better are occasionally used when blood pressure is very low due to poor heart function. Other intravenous drugs such as nitroglycerin and nesitiride reduce the pressure inside the left ventricle and reduce the symptoms of shortness of breath.

What measures can be taken to help reduce salt intake?

Too much sodium intake results in the body retaining water, which typically makes the symptoms of congestive heart failure worse. A common recommendation for total daily sodium intake is 2000 mg. Suggestions to help reduce salt intake include the following:

♥ Don't add salt to food during or after cooking; season foods with other flavorings such as pepper, onion, and garlic

♥ Eat low-salt snacks such as no-salt crackers and pretzels and air-popped popcorn

♥ Use sodium-free antacid tablets

♥ Read labels carefully when purchasing canned, processed, or frozen foods; many of these foods are high in salt content

♥ Use a cookbook containing many low-salt recipes

When should individuals with congestive heart failure get concerned enough to call their doctor's office?

When any of the following conditions exist, individuals should contact their doctor:

♥ Weight gain of 3 to 5 pounds (or more) in one week or 2 or more pounds in one day.

♥ Breathing becomes more difficult, especially if it occurs at rest or at night.

♥ Increasing fatigue and weakness.

♥ Increasing swelling in feet or ankles.

♥ Less frequent urination.

♥ New symptoms/side effects possibly related to medications (e.g., frequent dry cough from ACE inhibitor therapy).

 **Chapter 10**

Understanding Cardiomyopathy, or "Weak Heart Muscle"

Peter J. Sharis, MD

What is cardiomyopathy ("weak heart muscle") and how is it classified?

The *cardiomyopathies* are a group of diseases in which the primary feature is direct involvement and weakening of the heart muscle *(myocardium)* only. Cardiomyopathies are increasing in incidence and are a significant cause of death. *Dilated cardiomyopathy*, the most common type of cardiomyopathy, is reported to occur in 5 to 8 people per 100,000 population per year.

Cardiomyopathies occur more frequently in African Americans than whites and more commonly in men than women. Factors that are associated with increased death rates in cardiomyopathy patients include the following:

♥ *weak heart function* (left ventricular ejection fraction <35%)

♥ *aging* (i.e., age greater than 55 years)

♥ *reduced functional capacity*

♥ *electrical abnormalities*

♥ *low blood sodium level (hyponatremia)*

♥ *worsening kidney function*

Cardiomyopathy can be classified as ***primary***, which is ***heart muscle disease of unknown cause***, or ***secondary***, which is ***heart muscle disease due to specific causes*** (e.g., narrowing of the heart arteries, heart valve disease, high blood pressure).

The ***World Health Organization (WHO)*** classifies cardiomyopathy into three major groups:

♥ *dilated*
♥ *hypertrophic*
♥ *restrictive*

What are the features and causes of dilated cardiomyopathy?

Dilated cardiomyopathy (DCM) is typically characterized by significant enlargement of the two pumping chambers of the heart – the left ventricle (which pumps blood to the body) and the right ventricle (which pumps blood to the lungs). As a result of the chamber enlargement, there is some degree of reduction in the pumping power of the ventricle (***reduced ejection fraction***).

While there are many causes of dilated cardiomyopathy (nearly 80 specific diseases have been associated with DCM), a clear cause is often not identified in many individuals and these cases are described as ***idiopathic***. ***Alcohol abuse*** is a common cause of DCM as long-term ingestion leads to ***cardiac cell (myocyte) damage*** with subsequent heart dysfunction. Many patients can see significant improvement if they stop drinking. ***Cocaine abuse*** can lead to DCM in some individuals; in one large study, more than 10% of cocaine users had at least mild left ventricular dysfunction.

Infectious causes can also lead to dilated cardiomyopathy. *Viral infections* can attack the heart muscle and lead to significant cardiac dysfunction; in many cases, the damage can be irreversible and severe. In young adults, severe viral-related DCM is the top reason to be 'listed' for heart transplantation. *Human immunodeficiency virus (HIV)*, the cause of AIDS, can also lead to DCM in a minority of causes. Vitamin deficiencies (e.g., thiamine) can lead to dilated cardiomyopathy, though such cases occur more commonly in Third World countries.

Metabolic disorders can lead to dilated cardiomyopathy. One relatively common example is *hemochromatosis*, a disease of iron metabolism, which is often familial and more common in men, in which iron is deposited in the liver and heart muscle.

Peripartum cardiomyopathy is a form of DCM that typically occurs during the last 3 months of pregnancy and up to 6 months after delivery. It occurs in about 1 in every 5,000 pregnancies. The incidence is higher in women older than 30 years old and those with high blood pressure, multiple previous pregnancies, and twin pregnancies. Note that those who experience this condition are strongly discouraged from subsequent pregnancies, as the recurrence rate is high and death can even occur due to heart failure.

Chemotherapy drugs can lead to dilated cardiomyopathy in some individuals. Drugs most commonly associated with DCM are doxorubicin, cyclophosphamide, amsacrine, and interferon.

Neuromuscular disorders (i.e., *disorders of the muscles and nervous system)* are also associated with DCM.

Does therapy for dilated cardiomyopathy differ from that for congestive heart failure due to coronary artery disease (narrowing of the heart arteries)?

Treatment is similar for heart failure due to either dilated cardiomyopathy or coronary artery disease and includes:

- ♥ *Salt restriction, diuretics* (drugs that reduce lung and leg fluid via increased urine output)
- ♥ *Beta-blockers* (drugs which slow the heart rate and take stress off the heart),
- ♥ *Angiotensin-converting enzyme (ACE) inhibitors* (drugs which reduce the load on the heart by relaxing the body's major blood vessels)
- ♥ A combination of *hydralazine* and *isosorbide nitrates* (a drug option in those who cannot tolerate ACE inhibitors due to kidney function problems)
- ♥ *Digoxin* (a drug which helps improve the squeezing power of the heart)

What is hypertrophic cardiomyopathy (HCM)?

Hypertrophic cardiomyopathy (HCM) is a primary disorder of the heart muscle characterized by inappropriate *hypertrophy (excessive growth)* of the left ventricle, which is the chamber that pumps blood to the body's organs and tissues. In many individuals, hypertrophy predominantly involves the *septum*, which is the *intracardiac wall* that separates the left ventricle and right ventricle.

In at least one quarter of cases, this variant leads to obstruction of blood flow out of the left ventricle and into the *aorta*, and hence is called *hypertrophic obstructive cardiomyopathy (HOCM)*. Overall annual death rates in HCM individuals are approximately 3% per year in adults, while the rates are higher in those with HOCM.

What are the causes of hypertrophic cardiomyopathy (HCM)?

In more than 50% of cases, HCM is genetically transmitted. Most experts think that some if not all of the sporadic forms of HCM are due to *spontaneous mutations* (a sudden change in the genetic code of the developing fetus). At least eight different genes have been associated with HCM. Note that genetic testing is *not* currently indicated (except in research settings), even in families in which HCM occurs, because knowing the type of gene defect does not impact subsequent treatment.

What are the most frequent symptoms in patients with HCM?

Shortness of breath (dyspnea) occurs in approximately 90% of symptomatic individuals with HCM. It occurs due to a combination of abnormalities, including poor relaxation of the stiff, thickened heart muscle (*diastolic dysfunction*), reduced blood flow into the main heart pumping chamber (*impaired ventricular filling*), and increased pressures in the left atrium and pulmonary veins.

Fainting and near-fainting (syncope and near-syncope) can occur in HCM patients due to inadequate cardiac output during times of increased demand (e.g., physical exertion, severe stress). Serious *arrhythmias* can also result in fainting episodes; in fact, such arrhythmias are a top cause of sudden death in otherwise healthy children and young adults.

Chest pain (angina pectoris) occurs in up to three-fourths of symptomatic patients. The discomfort is a result of an imbalance between a reduced oxygen supply to the heart (because of thickened and narrowed heart arteries) and increased demand (due to greater heart muscle).

What noninvasive testing can be used to evaluate patients with suspected dilated cardiomyopathy or hypertrophic cardiomyopathy?

Useful tests include ***electrocardiography (ECG)***, ***chest x-ray***, and ***ultrasound (echocardiography)***.

In symptomatic individuals, the ECG is usually abnormal but no specific findings are diagnostic of either DCM or HCM.

A chest x-ray will demonstrate an enlarged cardiac silhouette in DCM patients and in some HCM patients.

An echocardiogram provides the most useful and specific information. In DCM patients, severe dilatation of the ventricles is demonstrated and an accurate estimation can be made of the impairment of heart function. In HCM patients, thickening of the left ventricle is the cardinal feature. Other findings include narrowing of the ***outflow tract*** through which blood flows from the left ventricle and out through the aortic valve and into the aorta, a small left ventricular cavity size, and abnormal motion of the ***mitral valve***.

101

What medical and invasive therapies are available to treat HCM patients?

Beta-blockers (examples: metoprolol, atenolol), which are drugs that slow down the heart rate, are the cornerstone of medical therapy for HCM. In up to two-thirds of patients, they reduce the frequency of chest pain, shortness of breath, and near fainting.

Calcium channel blockers (example: verapamil) have also been utilized with good success; they appear to help the thick heart muscle relax better (decreased diastolic dysfunction) and can reduce the outflow tract obstruction.

Insertion of a *pacemaker* may be useful in some patients with an outflow gradient and severe symptoms.

In high-risk patients, especially in those who have had serious ventricular arrhythmias or aborted sudden death, an *implantable cardiac defibrillator (ICD)* should be inserted.

Surgical and invasive options exist for severely symptomatic patients. A *surgical myomectomy*, or excision of excess heart muscle, has a mortality rate of 3% or less in large centers. Surgery results in long-term improvement in symptoms and exercise capacity in most patients.

A *non-surgical invasive approach* involves injection of alcohol into one of the arteries supplying the excessively thickened septal wall; this is done via left *catheterization* (small incision is made in a leg or arm artery to allow delivery of catheter into the specific artery under x-ray guidance). Short-term results in experienced centers have been promising, but long-term results are not yet available.

What is restrictive cardiomyopathy (RCM) and what are the most common forms?

Restrictive cardiomyopathy (RCM) – the least common of the cardiomyopathies – is characterized by abnormal relaxation of the heart muscle in the presence of normal ejection fraction. RCM is often classified into *myocardial* (throughout the heart muscle) and *endocardial* (from inside the ventricle).

The most common myocardial forms are *amyloidosis* and *sarcoidosis* (infiltrative diseases); *scleroderma* or *idiopathic* (noninfiltrative diseases); and *hemochromatosis*, *glycogen storage diseases*, and *Fabry's disease* (storage diseases).

Infiltrative diseases refer to abnormal proteins and cells generated by certain disease states that penetrate the heart muscle. *Noninfiltrative diseases* are typically diseases related to activation of the autoimmune system or due to a genetic abnormality that activates abnormal cardiac muscle growth, whereas the *storage diseases* refer to genetic abnormalities that lead to abnormal storage of sugars and other substances inside the heart muscle cells.

The most common endocardial forms of RCM are *carcinoid*, *metastatic malignancy* (spread of cancer), and *endomyocardial fibrosis*.

(For additional information, see Chapter 13 on details of the infiltrative diseases of the heart.)

 **Chapter 11**

Children and Heart Disease

Vickie Pyevich, MD

Is obesity in children a health concern?

My 10-year-old son is very self-conscious that he is overweight. At a recent physical exam, our physician told us that his blood pressure was also elevated. How concerned should we be about this?

Obesity in children is definitely a major health concern. Currently 1 in 5 U.S. children and adolescents are classified as overweight or at risk for being overweight. **Childhood obesity is now considered an epidemic related to many health conditions.** This includes cardiovascular disease such as hypertension, type II diabetes, and degenerative joint disease. Immediate childhood problems are also diagnosed in the obese child which require medical attention. High blood pressure is seen in 20-30% of overweight children. Sixty percent of overweight children ages 5-10 years old have at least one risk factor of future cardiovascular disease, such as increased blood pressure (hypertension), elevated cholesterol, and diabetes. Obstructive sleep apnea and other potentially life-threatening breathing difficulties can occur in obese children. Obesity also increases your child's risk for orthopedic problems such as hip disorders.

Obesity has important implications for the physical and psychosocial health of children. Boys and girls who view themselves as different from the "norm" often have poor self-esteem. Significant depression in overweight children has also been diagnosed. Furthermore, obese children are at higher risk of becoming obese adults and developing the chronic diseases associated with obesity in adulthood.

Currently 1 in 5 U.S. children and adolescents
are classified as overweight
or at risk for being overweight.

Research has shown that dietary habits and lifestyle patterns are established in early childhood. Published data from the National Institutes of Health (NIH) suggests a relationship between physical activity, hours of television viewing, a high-fat diet and high Body Mass Index (BMI). Obesity is significantly related to a sedentary lifestyle and a high-fat diet. Encouraging physical activity needs to be emphasized. A study of over 400 children ages 8-16 years old showed that 20% exercised vigorously twice per week or less. 67% of U.S. children watched TV more than two hours per day. This further suggests that TV viewing has replaced physical activity and thus is considered a link to obesity.

Increased physical activity has been associated with
an increase in life expectancy
and a decreased risk of cardiovascular disease.

105

So, should this mom worry about her child's obesity? The answer is "Yes," and your physician can help you in its treatment. Discuss this concern further with your health care provider. Consider introducing not only your child but your entire family to well-balanced meals rather than placing them on a "diet." Enroll your child in an after-school activity which will provide aerobic exercise such as basketball, soccer, swimming or tennis. Schedule "family time" into your weekends or after dinner that includes doing a fun physical activity. Making this lifestyle change as an entire family will be much more successful than focusing on the family member with the health risk. **Increased physical activity has been associated with an increase in life expectancy and a decreased risk of cardiovascular disease.**

It is easier to learn a healthy behavior
as a child
than as an adult.

Children are a reflection of their parents and thus will model their family's eating patterns. Busy lifestyles of many families leave little time for the traditional "family dinner" each evening. The alternative has become the fast food restaurant/drive-thru for a quick meal. Perhaps this environmental change contributes to the dramatic increase in obesity over the last two decades. Obesity is a risk factor to cardiovascular disease which we can address and hopefully minimize in our youth by educating them on proper nutrition and exercise.

Is chest pain in children a concern?

My 10-year-old daughter complains of chest pain while playing tennis. She also complains of chest discomfort at other times, such as watching TV or sitting doing her homework. Should I be concerned about this?

It is very scary for parents to hear that their child is having chest pain. It is natural to assume it could be the heart producing the discomfort. Many of us know of individuals who, when having a heart attack, complained of chest pain as their first symptom.

It is important to keep in mind that cardiac diseases seen in adults are very different from the cardiac problems seen in children. It is rare for a pediatric patient with chest pain to have an underlying heart defect. Most chest wall pain is due to *costochondritis*, or an inflammation of the cartilage, which attaches the ribs to the breastbone. Many children complain of this type of chest pain, especially if they are very active in sports, where a muscle sprain may have occurred. This type of pain is often accentuated by firm pressure over the site.

Other noncardiac causes of chest pain include stomach reflux, exercise-induced asthma, or pulmonary problems such as pneumonia. In this instance, typically other signs will be present, such as a fever and cough.

There are cardiac causes of chest pain, which should be evaluated by your physician. Typically, these serious causes of pain are associated with other symptoms as well. If your child appears pale or sweaty with the complaint of chest pain or reports being dizzy or passes out, you should immediately seek medical advice. Heart rhythm abnormalities and viral illnesses certainly can present with the above-described symptoms in children; hence it is important to contact your doctor if these symptoms occur in your child.

Should I screen my child for a cholesterol problem?

Because of my husband's history of elevated cholesterol our physician recommended that our children have their cholesterol levels screened. Is it common to detect elevated cholesterol values in children?

Cholesterol is a fat-like substance found in our blood and our body's cells. Cholesterol is packaged in proteins called *low-density lipoproteins (LDL)* and *high-density lipoproteins (HDL)*. HDL is considered the "good" cholesterol because it carries the "bad" LDL cholesterol back to the liver for removal. It is the LDL cholesterol that forms the plaque that builds up into the artery walls, increasing the risk of heart attacks.

Your son's cholesterol level can be related to his father's level. If a parent has high cholesterol, chances are that his or her children will have elevated values as well. Children with elevated blood cholesterol levels tend to have higher levels as they enter adulthood. Elevated cholesterol levels are a risk factor for heart disease. Heart disease is the number one killer of both men and women in the US. This is why your doctor needs to measure your child's cholesterol level.

If there is a family history of early cardiovascular disease such as stroke or heart attack under the age of 55 (this includes parent or grandparent), your child should be screened for ***familial hyperlipidemia***. This can be done by performing a fasting blood test. As is recommended by the American Academy of Pediatrics, we would consider treating children over the age of 10 years with elevated lipid screens, especially with a positive family history of early cardiovascular disease such as stroke or heart attack under the age of 55 years.

Many factors influence your blood cholesterol including your family's genes or family history. However, there are risk factors which you can control, such as activity level and eating patterns, both of which affect the blood cholesterol level. The amount of saturated fat and cholesterol in your diet and the cholesterol produced by your liver are reflected in the total cholesterol level. Obesity is associated with an increase in the total cholesterol level. Thus, regular aerobic activity five times per week will not only help control the weight but also reduce the fatty deposits of plaque in artery walls of children and adults, which lead to coronary artery disease. Striking evidence exists that fatty buildups in coronary arteries (***atherosclerosis***) begins in childhood especially if there are elevated cholesterol levels present.

As parents we need to live a healthy lifestyle and encourage our children to do the same. **It is easier to learn a healthy behavior as a child than as an adult.** This should be a family affair – one that will address many of the risk factors for heart disease and stroke.

The American Heart Association has made the following recommendations for selective screening of young children:

♥ Screen children whose parents or grandparents at 55 years of age or younger had been diagnosed with cardiovascular disease such as stroke or were found to have coronary atherosclerosis.

♥ Screen the offspring of a parent who has elevated cholesterol.

♥ Screen children whose family history is unknown or if there are other risk factors present which can affect the cholesterol level such as obesity, a sedentary lifestyle, and smoking.

Follow-up and treatment depends on the cholesterol level and family history of early cardiovascular disease. A total cholesterol level of 200 mg/dl or greater and LDL cholesterol of 130 mg/dl or greater are considered high in children. We do consider discussing initiating drug therapy in children over 10 years of age with worrisome family histories if diet and exercise therapy are not successful.

Weakness in the heart muscle: does it affect children?

I read in the paper that a fundraiser will be held for a previously healthy teenager who is now awaiting a heart transplant. The article described that a viral illness caused this heart infection. Is that common in a child?

This is known as *acquired heart disease* and refers to problems of the heart, which are not present at birth. Acquired weakness in the heart muscle is typically due to inflammation or infection of the heart muscle. *Viral myocarditis* is an infection of the heart due to a virus. Viruses that are related to the upper respiratory tract illnesses may infect the heart. The problem is very rare but does affect 1/100,000 children per year. It may be so severe that it results in significant heart damage necessitating a heart transplant.

"Blue Baby": Is this a concern?

My baby turns blue when he cries. Sometimes his hands and feet appear cool and purple. Does this mean he has a heart problem?

This is a very common finding in babies and is completely normal. The medical term used to describe this blueness is *acrocyanosis*. This word translated from its Greek roots means extremities *(acro)* + cyanosis *(blue)*. This results from immature vascular tone, which improves with age. The blood vessels in the hands and feet are constricting and thus slow the flow of blood, allowing more oxygen to be extracted from the hemoglobin by the surrounding tissues. It is a harmless condition seen in the newborn or infant when they are crying or even holding their breath. It's a normal response for the hands and feet to be cool in a baby, especially when they have no clothes on, such as while bathing or getting dressed.

Cyanosis means that a significant amount of the oxygen carrying protein in the blood, *hemoglobin*, is not carrying the oxygen it should. Cyanosis is divided into two types, *peripheral* or involving the extremities, as described above, and *central*. Central cyanosis (typically of the tongue and mouth) usually reflects decreased oxygen carrying due to lung or heart disease. Persistent cyanosis or blueness often indicates obstruction of blood flow to the lungs or an abnormal connection of the heart arteries. If your child appears blue throughout the day and limited in the ability to feed, you should discuss this with your doctor. This form of blueness may not be normal and should be evaluated by *pulse oximetry*, a painless test which measures the oxygen level in the blood and is readily available in your doctor's office. If the test is normal, peripheral cyanosis must be present.

Should I be concerned if my child faints?

My daughter fainted this morning while I was combing her hair. I remember fainting as a teenager while having my blood drawn. Should I call her physician?

Syncope, which is the medical term for *fainting*, is defined as a complete loss of consciousness and muscle tone for a very short period of time followed by a rapid, complete recovery. Syncope is a very common complaint affecting up to 15% of children and adolescents.

Fainting can be divided into cardiac and non-cardiac categories. The noncardiac cause of syncope can be thought of as the "common faint" and is typically benign, or not worrisome. It is more common than the other form of syncope, which is due to a serious cardiac problem. The physiological basis for the simple fainting is the decreased blood return to the heart, which stimulates nerve fibers that lead to a drop in heart rate, blood pressure or both.

There are many triggers of fainting, but the most common is prolonged standing. Pain, fear, the sight of blood, dehydration, illness and even temper tantrums may also provoke syncope, as we see in the toddler who has breath-holding spells. In the case above, the pain from scalp stimulation added to the fact that the child was standing during the grooming is a well-described cause of passing out.

The true heart causes of fainting are due to decreased blood flow out of the heart or perhaps from a rhythm abnormality. These may result in sudden death. In these patients, a history of prior fainting, especially with exercise, is common. If there is a history of a known underlying structural heart problem or a rhythm abnormality in a patient with syncope, immediate medical attention should be sought.

Your physician may consult with a pediatric cardiologist for further evaluation of your child's syncope. Special tests may be ordered, such as an electrocardiogram, which assesses the heart rhythm. For the common faint, the treatment strategy is aimed at increasing fluid and salt intake. Typically this is a self-limiting problem which improves gradually over time.

What is a fetal echocardiogram?

I am 30 weeks pregnant. During a recent obstetrical exam, my physician noted that my baby's heart rate was irregular. She is sending me for a fetal echocardiogram. Is this harmful to my baby?

An irregular heartbeat is often detected *in utero*, especially in the third trimester. Normal fetal heart rate is between 120 and 160 bpm (beats per minute). A sustained rhythm of over 200 bpm is of concern. Most often the irregular rhythm is a normal finding and does not imply structural heart disease in the fetus. However, the rhythm would be evaluated to detect serious heart rhythm

113

abnormalities.

An occasional early fetal heartbeat with a structurally normal fetal heart is nothing to worry about. These early beats will disappear close to delivery or within the first month or so of life. These early beats originate from the upper chambers of the heart a little sooner than normal, but if isolated and infrequent, they are of no significance. They are not treated with medications.

Frequent early beats known as *PACs* or *premature atrial contractions* are very rarely (1%) associated with a very fast heart rhythm problem is known as *SVT or supraventricular tachycardia*. This condition can be detected in utero and treated by giving the mother special medications. At times the fast heart rate is so frequent that the fetal heart enlarges and does not contract or squeeze effectively. Occasionally delivery is then induced to be able to more effectively treat the baby's heart rhythm abnormality.

An abnormally slow heart rate where the upper and lower heart chambers do not communicate is known as *complete heart block*, or *CHB*. A fetal heart rate between 60 – 80 bpm is usually well-tolerated by the baby. A rhythm less than 60 bpm with a congenital heart defect is not. Certain maternal conditions, such as lupus, have been associated with CHB. Also there is a high association of congenital heart disease with CHB and this unfortunately suggests a poor outcome for the fetus.

What is an innocent heart murmur?

Our child was recently diagnosed with an innocent heart murmur. What is an innocent murmur and is it serious?

A *murmur* is simply a sound heard with the stethoscope of the blood traveling through the chambers and valves of the heart. Certain murmurs heard in children are suggestive of structural heart disease, though the vast majority of murmurs heard in children are truly "innocent" or nothing to worry about. An *innocent murmur,* also known as a *physiologic* or *vibratory murmur*, has a very characteristic sound and does not imply a heart defect.

These innocent murmurs may become louder during times of fever, illness or stress. This is a normal finding in the innocent murmur. Innocent murmurs are often noted in the child between the ages of 2 and 5 yrs old. They are so common that at least 80% of all children are felt to have had one at some point in time. They often come and go. Thus, your doctor may hear the murmur during one exam and then not detect it on a follow-up visit. Many innocent murmurs disappear as the children grow up.

Often your child's doctor may want to have the murmur evaluated by a children's heart doctor (*pediatric cardiologist*). The cardiologist may want to perform an *electrocardiogram* and chest x-ray. These are helpful to the doctor in determining the innocence or guilt of the murmur. If the cardiologist was concerned that the murmur may not be innocent, then he or she would consider performing an ultrasound known as an echocardiogram. This very safe, non-invasive test provides detailed pictures of your child's heart and can thus confirm or refute congenital heart disease.

Once the murmur is deemed innocent or "normal," there is no need to have any further cardiac testing. No physical activity restrictions should be placed on your child. Your child will not have any symptoms from this murmur, nor will he or she require cardiac medications. Your child's heart is healthy and you should not worry about the murmur detected.

How does Kawasaki disease affect the heart in children?

Our daughter was recently diagnosed with Kawasaki's disease. Will this lead to serious long-term heart problems?

Kawasaki's disease, also known as **mucocutaneous lymph node syndrome**, is primarily a childhood illness diagnosed not by a single laboratory test but by history and clinical examination.

The children are very irritable. They have high fevers lasting over 5 days, a rash, swelling of the hands and feet, with eventual peeling of the skin, red, blood-shot eyes (**conjunctivitis**), swollen lymph nodes in the neck and red and swollen mouth, lips and throat. Long-term cardiac complications of the disease can occur, especially if the diagnosis is not made promptly and thus treatment is delayed.

A Japanese pediatrician, Dr. Tomisaku Kawasaki, originally identified the disease in 1961. It is more frequent in the Asian or Asian-American child but can occur in any racial group. In the U.S., there are 6000 children affected each year. 80% of the cases are in children less than 5 years of age, with the average age of diagnosis being 2 years old. Boys are affected almost twice as often as girls.

The cause of Kawasaki's disease is unknown. There is no evidence that the disease is transmitted from person to person. We do know that it is an intense inflammatory disease, which can affect the coronary arteries, which are the blood vessels that supply the heart muscle as well as the heart muscle itself. The coronary arteries can weaken and aneurysms or discrete swelling of the artery may develop and this could be life threatening if not treated appropriately.

Though a single blood test cannot diagnose Kawasaki's disease, various blood tests are performed primarily to eliminate other diseases which may mimic Kawasaki's disease. An *echocardiogram* (ultrasound of the heart) is performed within the first couple days of when the diagnosis is made to assess for heart function and the anatomy of the coronary arteries, specifically to determine if coronary artery aneurysms have developed. A follow-up echocardiogram is performed roughly 6 weeks after the initial echocardiogram to screen for any late-developing cardiac involvement.

Treatment includes a brief hospital stay with administration of a special intravenous medication known as *gamma globulin*. This medication has been proven to decrease the incidence of the life-threatening, long-term heart problems with the coronary arteries which can occur in the child with Kawasaki's disease. The children are also treated with high-dose aspirin therapy until the fever has completely resolved. The majority of children who are treated with gamma globulin during the first 10 days of illness recover completely.

How concerned should I be if my child complains of fluttering in the chest?

Our 10-year-old daughter is complaining of periodic episodes of a fast heart rate, lasting several minutes, sometimes associated with chest pain. At times, she feels the fast heart rate while playing. Could this be normal?

It is not uncommon for children to be aware of an increase in their heart rate while playing. This is a normal response of heart rate to activity.

Heart rate is clearly age-dependent. A newborn's average heart rate could be 150 bpm while the teenager's average heart rate could be 70 beats per minute. The heart rate can easily change. Exercise will increase the rate, and sleeping is when the heart rate will be at its lowest. An irregular heartbeat (***arrhythmia***) most often is a normal finding in an otherwise healthy child. Heart rate irregularity typically occurs while breathing. Sometimes irregularities are noted which are not normal and thus a pediatric cardiologist may be consulted.

An unusually fast heart rate is called a ***tachycardia***. Tachycardia comes form the Greek word "tachy" *(fast)* and "cardia" *(heart)*. As mentioned, a heart rate depends upon the child's age as well as activity. A 10-year-old with a heart rate over 200 bpm may or may not be normal. A 10- year-old's heart rate greater than 280 bpm is certainly not normal and requires prompt medical attention. This extremely fast heart rate, known as ***SVT***, or ***supraventricular tachycardia***, typically is not life-threatening and does not always require medication for its resolution.

SVT develops because of an abnormal electrical connection in the child's heart. It may appear in the fetal period or not until adolescence. When it occurs, the older child may complain of dizziness, chest pain and report that they are very scared. Many children report that it feels as thought the heart is about to jump out of their chest.

Your physician may order a special test to further characterize the fast heart rate or irregular rhythm your child describes. A small recorder may be sent home with your child, which can be used for 30 days to capture the rhythm of concern. The recorder is activated during your child's symptoms. The information can then be transferred over your telephone to the cardiologist for interpretation.

If an abnormally fast rhythm is detected, treatment options are available. They include oral medication or a procedure called ***radio frequency catheter ablation***. In this procedure performed by a pediatric cardiologist specializing in childhood rhythm abnormalities, known as an ***electrophysiologist***, a catheter is positioned over the abnormal electrical pathway and energy is applied to permanently eliminate the tachycardia.

What is a "hole" in the heart?

Our child was born with a hole in the heart. What exactly is this and why did this happen? Is it likely that I will have another child with a heart defect?

Eight out of every 1000 children are born with congenital heart disease, most of which are mild cases. Congenital heart defects are structural abnormalities of the heart, which occurred during the baby's development in the womb. Severe congenital heart disease is the No. 1 cause of death in infants. Fortunately, the overall death rate from congenital heart disease is dramatically improving, which can be attributed to the earlier recognition of the defects and advances in surgical techniques and post-operative care.

A hole in the bottom chambers of the heart is a *ventricular septal defect*, or *VSD*. It is the most common of all birth defects. Many VSDs require no treatment. Often the small defects close spontaneously, typically by the age of three. These holes do not become larger as the child grows.

Up until recently the cause of congenital heart defects was thought to be *multifactorial* – that is, due to many reasons with little known genetic cause. We now think that up to 27% of heart defects are associated with chromosomal abnormalities, which perhaps are inherited. A very recent genetic study has identified specific gene abnormalities within affected family members with similar heart defects of an *upper chamber hole*, or *atrial septal defect*. There are genetic syndromes, such as *Down syndrome*, which have associated cardiac defects. There are also environmental exposures associated with congenital heart disease. Examples of this are certain medications for acne, seizures or psychiatric illnesses. Viral infections during pregnancy or specific maternal conditions such as diabetes or lupus are associated with a higher risk of congenital heart disease. Of course, alcohol consumption and the use of street drugs are linked to structural defects of the heart.

Once there is a history of congenital heart disease in the family, the risk of recurrence does increase in subsequent pregnancies. The chance of recurrence is anywhere from 2-8 %. Mothers with a family history of congenital heart disease should undergo a specialized cardiac ultrasound of the fetus at roughly 20 weeks of pregnancy. This very safe test, known as a *fetal echocardiogram*, is performed by a pediatric cardiologist. This study can detect serious heart defects, which would require the baby to be delivered at a specialized children's heart center where appropriate immediate medical treatment could be obtained.

Exercise is important for all children, including those with congenital heart disease. We promote healthy lifestyles for children with heart defects, which include maintaining a good weight. Often we will individualize physical activities such as PE class for children with certain congenital heart disease.

Children with complex defects are easily fatigued with competitive activities. These children recognize their limitations and thus learn to self-limit their activity. Our overall strategy as pediatric cardiologists is to incorporate age-appropriate activities and to "normalize" lifestyle as much as possible.

 **Chapter 12**

Diseases of the Pericardium

Edmund O. Fiksinski, MD, FACC

What is the pericardium?

The *pericardium* is a thin but strong fibrous sac which envelops the heart *(see Figure 1)*. The pericardium is attached to the portion of the great blood vessels in the chest, the diaphragm and the central breastbone. The space between the inner and outer layer of the pericardium is filled with a small amount of lubricating fluid. The amount of fluid that can be accommodated within the space is quite small, usually less than one-third of a cup. The pericardium maintains an optimal position of the heart within the chest throughout the cycle of respirations, protects the heart from infections, and prevents sudden enlargement and stretching of the heart chambers.

What are the most common diseases affecting the pericardium?

By far the most common process affecting the pericardium is *pericarditis*, an inflammation in the lining of the heart. Other diseases, including benign and malignant tumors, are much less frequent.

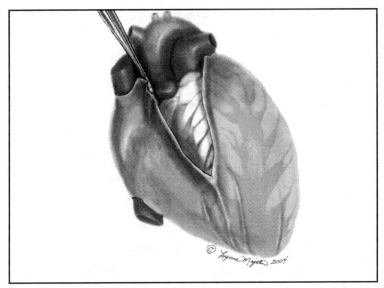

Figure 1. Pericardium.

What is pericarditis and how is it caused?

Pericarditis is an inflammatory process involving both the inner and outer layer of the pericardium. It can be viewed as a reaction of the pericardium to a variety of different factors.

The most common cause of pericarditis is *viral infection*. It can be a consequence of viral infection in children. Some of the viruses are the same as those that cause common respiratory infections. A typical patient with acute pericarditis is a young man who recently suffered respiratory infection. It is also seen among the patients infected with HIV virus.

Bacterial infections involving the pericardium are infrequent and usually result from a source of infection elsewhere in the body. Sometimes pericarditis follows chest surgery.

123

In the past, *tuberculosis* was a common cause of pericarditis. These days, with effective anti-tuberculosis therapy widely available, *tuberculosis pericarditis* occurs usually in patients with a weakened defense system (for example, cancer or HIV patients).

There are many other potential causes of pericarditis, including *trauma*, *kidney failure*, *hypothyroidism* (insufficient production of thyroid hormone), *cancer* (most frequently breast, lung and blood) and some *medications*, including hydralazine, procainamide, isoniazid, reserpine, and methyldopa. Orally but not topically used *minoxidil* has been reported to cause pericarditis. *Radiation to the chest* may also cause pericardial inflammation and is related to the dose duration as well as the quality of the technical equipment. It may occur during or following radiation therapy. Pericarditis is one of the possible complications of *heart attack*.

What are the symptoms of pericarditis?

The typical symptom of pericarditis is chest pain associated with fever and feeling sick. The pain is usually sharp, located in the center and the left side of the chest, often spreading to the neck and the left shoulder. The pain is made worse by deep breathing or swallowing. It is relieved with sitting. A dry cough, hiccups and breathing difficulty may be present. *It is extremely important for any person with chest pain to seek immediate professional attention.*

How is pericarditis diagnosed?

The diagnosis is established based on the characteristic pain and the presence of a typical crackling sound called *pericardial rub*, frequently compared to the sound of walking in the snow. An EKG is frequently abnormal and shows characteristic changes. Other laboratory tests may be helpful and frequently include blood counts, blood cultures, erythrocyte sedimentation rate (ESR) and C-reactive protein. Additional tests for pericarditis include chest x-ray, echocardiogram and heart MRI or CT scan.

How is pericarditis treated?

The treatment of pericarditis begins with identification of its *etiology* (that is, its cause). The usual case of pericarditis caused by a viral infection is treated with pain killers and medications designed to reduce the inflammation, such as aspirin, ibuprofen, or indomethacin. Other medications and in some cases steroids may be required.

Even if you suspect pericarditis, it is extremely important to be seen by a health professional to have the diagnosis confirmed. Sometimes a heart attack may feel similar to pericarditis, and in such a case, any delay in therapy can have profound consequences. Pericarditis caused by other factors mentioned above may require a different approach. For example, bacterial infection is treated with antibiotics and surgical drainage.

What are some of the complications of pericarditis?

The most common complication of pericarditis is *tamponade*, an excessive accumulation of fluid between the two layers of the pericardium, leading to compression and impaired function of the pumping heart chamber. It can be life-threatening and requires immediate attention. The treatment in this case is *pericardiocentesis*, which involves drainage of the pericardial fluid with a needle. Surgical drainage may be required in cases where needle aspiration is ineffective.

How is pericardiocentesis performed?

Pericardiocentesis, or *pericardial tap,* is frequently performed in the patient's room at the bedside or in a specialized procedure room called the Cardiac Catheterization Laboratory. The area below the breastbone is cleaned with an antiseptic solution and a local anesthetic agent is administered. Intravenous sedation is often given to improve the patient's cooperation. A needle is then introduced just below the breastbone under the guidance of an electrocardiogram (EKG) or an echocardiogram utilizing sound waves to visualize the heart structures. Once the needle is within the pericardial space, a guide wire is placed through the needle and the needle is then exchanged for a plastic catheter. This catheter is then connected to a container which will collect the fluid.

The catheter is often left within the pericardium for several hours and sometimes even a few days. The needle passage into the pericardium may provoke a feeling of pressure. Less frequently the patient experiences transient pain, which may require additional pain medication.

Complications of this procedure may include bleeding, penetrating trauma to one of the heart chambers, irregular heart rhythm, puncture of the surrounding organs, and infection. Fortunately, these complications occur exceedingly rarely. However, when present, they may require surgical correction.

Can pericarditis cause long-term problems?

The most common long-term complication of pericarditis is *constrictive pericarditis*, which occurs when the inflammation within the pericardial sac leads to scarring of the two layers of the pericardium and turns them into a stiff, leather-like case. This limits the heart's ability to fill up with blood and leads to symptoms of progressive shortness of breath, weakness and leg swelling. Constrictive pericarditis is treated with surgical removal of the pericardium.

What is the prognosis in a typical case of pericarditis?

Many cases of pericarditis resolve (that is, heal) spontaneously or with treatment involving common anti-inflammatory medications. Most patients improve within a few weeks. In some people the disease recurs within months to a year, sometimes repeatedly. The treatment is usually similar to the original therapy. Some of the other medications used for recurrent cases include colchicine. Surgical creation of an opening within the pericardium (*pericardial window*) is occasionally required and allows for free drainage absorption of the fluid.

What kinds of tumors can affect the pericardium?

The pericardium may be affected by benign and malignant tumors – however, these conditions are very uncommon. On occasion, a cyst may develop within the pericardium and is usually found in middle-aged men and women. Some patients may present with symptoms of chest discomfort, shortness of breath or heart rhythm irregularities. Diagnosis is typically confirmed with an echocardiogram, MRI or a CAT scan. Treatment requires surgical resection, although some cases of successful needle aspirations have been reported as well.

A malignant tumor of the pericardium is called *mesothelioma*. It is very rare and linked to long-term asbestos exposure. It usually takes over 15 years for this form of cancer to occur, and in its early stages it can be easily missed. Symptoms – such as chest pain, cough and shortness of breath – frequently can be misleading. A diagnosis is often suggested by a CAT scan or MRI but is frequently made in the late stages of the disease. Since mesothelioma is one of the most aggressive cancers, the treatment is often ineffective and is usually aimed at the relief of symptoms. Chemotherapy or radiation therapy is sometimes used. New treatments are currently being studied and may become available in the next several years.

What is the most important thing to remember about pericardial disease?

Do not try to self-diagnose yourself with pericarditis. Do not use anti-inflammatory medications for chest discomfort. **It is extremely important for any person with chest pain to seek immediate professional attention.** Remember, in American society, heart attack is still the No. 1 killer.

 ***Chapter 13***

Systemic Illnesses, Infections and Drugs that Affect the Heart

Moutasim H. Al-Shaer, MD

Can Lyme disease affect the heart?

Lyme disease is an infection that affects multiple body systems caused by an organism called *Borrelia burgdorferi*. Ticks that exist in certain areas of the United States transmit the disease. This infection goes through three stages. In the first stage, people usually experience rash and flu-like symptoms. The second stage is when the disease affects the heart and other organs. The third stage is usually the arthritis stage.

During the second stage, 8% of the people affected experience heart involvement, which happens within the first two months of the infection. For some this involvement is not apparent, but others may complain of being lightheaded, short of breath, having a fast heartbeat, chest pain or passing out.

A variety of heart rhythm abnormalities occur, ranging from simple problems to those requiring a pacemaker.

The most common manifestation of the disease is infection of the heart muscle. This is usually temporary and presents as an enlargement of the heart due to fluids in the sac around the heart. This fluid might appear on a chest X-ray or an ultrasound of the heart. In some rare cases these effects may last a long time.

Antibiotics are usually administered to treat this condition, although there is no strong evidence to support that this treatment facilitates the improvement of heart disease. These antibiotics are given either by mouth or through the veins (intravenous). Oral antibiotics are usually given in mild cases, whereas patients with symptoms of passing out or light-headedness are usually admitted to the hospital, where they are monitored and given intravenous antibiotics.

With adequate treatment and monitoring, patients usually experience a good outcome. The rhythm problems usually resolve spontaneously within two to three months, although sometimes patients might need a pacemaker for a short period.

Can Systemic Lupus Erythematosus (SLE) affect the heart?

SLE (*Lupus*) is an *autoimmune disease* (a disease where the immune system attacks the person's own organs). Most patients with lupus experience periods of increased and decreased disease activity. This disease affects multiple organs in the body, including the joints, heart, skin, kidneys, blood and spleen.

Lupus affects the heart in almost 75% of the patients. Usually the most commonly affected are the heart valves. The pattern of involvement of the valves includes thickening, valve growths, or problems with leaking or narrowed valves. This involvement might worsen or resolve during the course of the disease, and might lead to scarring of the heart valves.

The *pericardium* (sac of the heart) is the second most commonly affected part of the heart. The sac could either be inflamed and irritated (*pericarditis*) or filled with fluids (*pericardial effusion*). In addition, inflammation of the heart muscle (*myocarditis*) can occur.

Problems with the heart rhythm can occur but are usually mild. Increased heart rate has been shown to be an indicator of increased disease activity.

Patients with lupus have accelerated plaque buildup in their arteries (*atherosclerosis*). This might be caused by the increased presence of high blood pressure, cholesterol abnormalities, vessel injury from the autoimmune process, increased blood tendency to form clots, sedentary lifestyle caused by arthritis, or medications used to treat the lupus.

Patients with lupus suffer from involvement of multiple organs and body systems, making heart complications only one part of the disease process. Usually the affliction of the heart is not the major cause of sickness and death in these patients.

Can Sarcoidosis affect the heart?

Sarcoidosis is a disease of unknown origin that affects multiple systems within the body. It usually affects young and middle-aged individuals. The disease presents with cough, shortness of breath, night sweats, fatigue, and skin changes.

Approximately 80% of individuals with the disease experience spontaneous disappearance of the disease within two years.

Cardiac sarcoidosis (sarcoidosis affecting the heart) can be a benign or a life-threatening disorder.

Heart involvement may happen before, during, or after sarcoidosis affects the lung. The most common effect on the heart is electrical disturbance (***arrhythmia***). This usually starts without symptoms but may progress and even require a pacemaker.

Rhythm problems occur in as many as one fifth of patients with sarcoidosis. Of the people with sarcoidosis who develop rhythm problems, sometimes these rhythms progress to types that might lead to sudden death. The mild forms of rhythm problems are usually evident on the electrocardiogram early in the course of this disease.

Heart failure (weakening of the heart muscle) may occur when the muscle is invaded with ***granulomas*** (a group of cells that are caused by sarcoidosis). Sometimes the granulomas invade the muscles that control heart valves motion. This may lead to leakage of the heart valves.

When the granulomas invade the heart muscle, an alteration in the appearance of the electrocardiogram results, and this might be mistaken for a heart attack.

Sarcoidosis commonly affects the lungs, leading to stiffness of the lungs and increased pressure inside them. This lung involvement can lead to excess pressure on the right side of the heart (***Cor pulmonale***).

Rarely the pericardium (the heart sac) is affected by sarcoidosis, although it may become inflamed, giving rise to ***pericarditis*** (inflammation of the heart sac).

133

What is the effect of HIV infection on the heart?

Human Immunodeficiency Virus (HIV) is a germ (*retrovirus*) that infects the blood cells responsible for the body's defense against foreign organisms. Immunity against infections is reduced in patients with HIV. People with HIV have more serious infections than healthy people.

With new advances in the treatment of HIV infection, people infected with this virus are living longer and therefore heart manifestations of this infection are more apparent.

HIV-infected people can have a variety of heart diseases. *Pericarditis* (inflammation of the heart sac) is the most frequent of these complications, and when it is associated with a *pericardial effusion* (fluid in the heart sac), it can become a serious complication.

HIV can also affect the heart muscle, ranging from an inflammation to weakening and dilation of the heart chambers.

Pulmonary hypertension (increased pressure in the lungs) may occur because HIV patients get a number of lung infections that lead to scarring and increased stiffness of the lungs.

Heart tumors are usually rare in the general population, but they happen at an increased frequency in HIV-infected people. *Kaposi's sarcoma* is the tumor that usually affects people with HIV infection. It may affect the heart itself or the sac of the heart.

Infection and damage of the heart valves also might occur. However, with the presence of an impaired immune system, it is more difficult to treat.

134

HIV-infected people are sometimes treated with medications called Protease Inhibitors, which are effective but may sometimes lead to increased cholesterol and have also been linked to accelerated plaques in the arteries of the heart. It has been noted that people with HIV infection are more likely to develop heart attacks than healthy individuals, a problem that might be related to the disease itself or the medications used to treat it.

As for the blood vessels of the legs, it was found that HIV-infected people suffer from more frequent blood clots (*venous thrombosis*).

What are the effects of sleep apnea on the heart?

Sleep apnea occurs in 4% of men and 2% of women, most commonly between the ages of 30 to 60. Common symptoms of sleep apnea include loud snoring, disrupted sleep, daytime sleepiness, repetitive awakening, mood disturbances, decreased drive to perform sex, morning headaches, poor memory, impaired concentration, night sweats and morning dry mouth. Individuals with this problem are usually obese with a large neck circumference. However, not all these symptoms and signs are diagnostic for sleep apnea. The definitive test for sleep apnea is a *sleep study*. This condition is becoming more recognized to the extent that some teams in the NFL are screening their players and offering treatment to improve their performance.

Sleep apnea is a disease that is becoming more common because of the alarming increase in the percentage of overweight individuals.

Individuals suffering from sleep apnea experience repetitive changes in the blood pressure and heart function during the night. It has long been noted that individuals with sleep apnea are likely to suffer from hypertension (high blood pressure). It is likely that they also have more plaque buildup in their arteries, leading to frequent chest pains or even heart attacks.

Heart rhythm problems are frequent. Commonly these individuals will experience slowness of the heart rate and even ventricular *asystole* (electrical silence of the heart). Electrical disturbances of the heart have been described with sleep apnea.

Recent reports have correlated sleep apnea with heart failure. Moreover, treatment of sleep apnea was shown to improve hypertension and overall well-being of the people with this problem.

Treatment of sleep apnea includes weight reduction and continuous positive airway pressure *(CPAP)* therapy to help with the breathing problems and minimize the harmful effects of reduced oxygenation on the body.

Can thyroid disease affect the heart?

The *thyroid* gland is a butterfly-shaped gland in the neck. It has two lobes and it resides around the breathing pipe (*trachea*). The thyroid gland produces a hormone (*thyroxine*) that regulates the body's consumption of energy (*metabolism*).

When the thyroid gland does not produce enough thyroxine (*hypothyroidism*), there is generalized slowness of the body functions. This common condition is five to ten times more common in females. Common presentations include cold intolerance, fatigue, weight gain, constipation, dry skin, muscle cramps, and increased menstrual bleeding. The effects of hypothyroidism on the heart include: decreased heart rate (***bradycardia***), irregular heart rhythm and heart failure. Hypothyroidism can also raise the cholesterol and homocysteine levels, both linked to developing atherosclerotic plaques in the coronaries.

The treatment of hypothyroidism is replacing the thyroid hormone in the form of a pill.

In contrast, increased secretion of thyroxine (***hyperthyroidism***) is a less common disorder. The usual presentations of this disorder include weight loss, increased appetite, heat intolerance, excessive sweating, flushing, restlessness, shakiness (tremors), and mood changes. As for the heart effects of hyperthyroidism, these include a fast heartbeat (***palpitations***), increased blood pressure, and irregular heartbeats. Individuals with established coronary artery disease might experience chest pains. Also elderly individuals with hyperthyroidism might develop heart failure and an irregular heart beat involving the top chambers of the heart (***atrial fibrillation***).

The treatment of hyperthyroidism is to surgically or by drugs remove the active areas of the thyroid gland that are hyperproducing the thyroid hormone.

How does obesity affect the heart?

Obesity is a growing health concern. In 1999, the National Health and Nutrition Examination Survey (NHANES) estimated an alarming 61 percent of U.S. adults are either overweight or obese. Being obese means that the individual's body fat is excessively high.

Several methods exist to define the extent of obesity and to correlate it with increased risk. Common simple methods include ***BMI*** (***body mass index***), waist circumference and waist-hip ratio. Other measurements also exist, and there are ways to measure the fat distribution by using radiological methods (X-ray).

A useful and simple method to find out if you are obese, overweight or within the normal range is to measure BMI. BMI can be calculated from the weight and height using a mathematical formula, and could be easily done by accessing tables and calculators on the internet (http://nhlbisupport. com/bmi/bmicalc.htm).

Generally, if your BMI is 18.5 or below you are considered underweight; a normal BMI is within the range of 18.5 – 24.9; you are considered overweight if your BMI is 25.0 – 29.9; and if your BMI is 30.0 and above, then you are obese.

Obesity is an established risk factor for coronary disease (narrowing and blockages of the heart arteries leading to angina and heart attacks), hypertension (high blood pressure), sleep apnea, enlargement of the heart, and heart failure.

It commonly affects the lipid profile (fat in the blood) by decreasing HDL (good cholesterol) and increasing triglycerides. It can also cause heart rhythm abnormalities.

C-reactive protein, an emerging risk factor of heart disease, is higher in obese individuals.

Studies have shown an improvement in lipid profiles, blood pressure, symptoms of sleep apnea, heart failure and improved life expectancy from weight loss. Weight loss is best achieved by a balanced diet and an exercise regimen.

If you are over 40 years of age, consult with your doctor to evaluate you for readiness to start an exercise program (psychological and physical). Also, your doctor and a qualified dietitian may offer you great help in choosing the right dietary regimen for you.

What are the effects of alcohol on the heart?

Moderate alcohol consumption reduces the risk of coronary heart disease. People who consumed an average of five drinks per week had the lowest risk of coronary artery disease. There is controversy regarding the kind of alcohol that you should drink to lower your coronary heart disease risk. Some studies advocate red wine, but others found no difference in the kind of alcohol consumed.

Whereas a moderate amount of alcohol intake may protect the heart, chronic high alcohol intake increases the incidence of *hypertension* (high blood pressure), *heart failure*, and *cardiomyopathy* (weakness of the heart muscle)

Alcohol cardiomyopathy (weakness of the heart muscle related to alcohol) is caused by habitual excessive intake of alcohol. This condition leads to the development of heart failure. Heavy alcohol intake may cause this condition through inducing a deficiency of vitamins or through a direct effect of alcohol on the heart muscle.

Holiday heart syndrome is a condition that happens to people who binge-drink on the holidays and weekends. It is a condition where binge drinkers experience heart rhythm abnormalities after a heavy episode of drinking.

As for the effects on cholesterol, moderate alcohol intake causes an increase in HDL (good cholesterol), but it also increases the serum triglycerides (a type of fat in the blood).

Although alcohol intake might have some beneficial effects on the heart, it also has harmful effects on the heart and other body systems such as the liver and the brain. **If you are not a drinker, the current recommendation is not to start.**

Can marijuana affect the heart?

Marijuana use is an increasing problem. The plant *Cannabis sativa* is the source of marijuana. The most common route of use is smoking the dried leaves. It is the most commonly used illegal drug in the United States. Marijuana is a serious problem because it is considered less risky than other drugs and it is cheaper.

As for the effect on the heart, marijuana causes fast heart rate (*tachycardia*), which might lead to irregular heart rhythm and may increase blood pressure.

Because of the spreading use of marijuana and the fact that some people use it on an habitual basis, it has been recognized that the repeated inhalation of marijuana smoke is harmful to the lungs and may eventually lead to heart disease.

Marijuana is sometimes used in combination with other illicit drugs, many of which have serious harmful effects on the heart.

The use of marijuana in people with underlying heart disease worsens their condition and might increase the chance of heart attacks.

What are the dangers of cocaine on the heart?

Cocaine is the second most commonly used illegal drug in the United States. This drug can lead to heart disease whether it is used only once or repeatedly over a long period. Cocaine users commonly present to the emergency room because of heart complications.

Heart attack is the most serious complication of cocaine use, and it can occur even in young individuals. This drug causes an increase in the heart rate and blood pressure. This complication can occur irrespective of the route of use.

Cocaine can induce *myocarditis* (an inflammation of the heart muscle) and it is a common finding on autopsy in individuals dying from cocaine abuse.

Cocaine can also cause *cardiomyopathy* (weakness of the heart muscle), which eventually leads to heart failure.

Cocaine might induce *bradycardia* (slow heart rate), *tachycardia* (fast heart rate), and a variety of heart rhythm problems including heart blocks (the inability of the electrical impulse to travel from the top to the bottom chambers of the heart).

Individuals who use cocaine by intravenous injections are at risk to develop infection of the heart valves (*endocarditis*).

Crack cocaine use can result in an internal tear of the lining of the *aorta* (the main artery that comes out of the heart). This is a very serious and many times deadly condition.

Besides these serious heart conditions, intravenous use of cocaine increases the risk of infections, including HIV.

What are the effects of Amyloidosis on the heart?

Amyloidosis is a disease that results from deposition of certain types of proteins in different organs of the body.

Amyloidosis is either a primary disease, meaning it is a stand-alone disease affecting around 5-10 people per million per year, or a secondary disease, meaning it is a complication of another disease, like tuberculosis or rheumatoid arthritis.

Multiple systems of the body are affected. These include the lungs, kidneys, heart, glands, gastrointestinal system (gut), muscles, bones, nerves and brain.

When amyloidosis affects the heart, it could lead to various complications. *Amyloid cardiomyopathy* happens when this protein invades the heart muscle. This leads to weakening of the heart muscle, which precipitates heart failure.

The involvement of the heart muscle and conduction system (the electrical wiring of the heart) leads to heart rhythm diseases and could even lead to sudden death. The rhythm problem could be a fast one or a slow one.

In addition to directly affecting the heart, amyloidosis also affects other organ systems as mentioned above, which makes the heart condition difficult to treat.

Amyloidosis is a rare disease and the treatment consists mostly of treating the complications and symptoms. Currently no curative treatment exists.

How can Pharyngitis affect the heart?

Pharyngitis is an inflammation of the pharynx (throat) caused by an infection. This infection is usually viral or bacterial. It usually manifests as sore and red throat, enlarged tonsils and lymph nodes and fever. Sometimes the infecting organism results in a condition called *scarlet fever*, which usually involves sore throat, skin rash and a white-coated tongue that changes to shiny red in a few days.

When bacteria (typically *streptococcus*) cause this infection, there is a potential for a secondary complication called *rheumatic fever*. Rheumatic heart disease can be one complication of rheumatic fever and results in destruction of the heart valves. Rheumatic fever is often a recurrent condition and is preventable by antibiotic treatment.

Rheumatic fever manifests as a combination of one or more of the following: arthritis (pain in the joints), inflammation of the heart and its valves, changes in mental status, and skin rash.

Carditis (inflammation of the heart) involves the whole heart and causes chest pain. In addition to carditis, inflammation of the heart valves may lead to narrowing or leakage of the heart valves. Valve damage may persist beyond the acute episode of rheumatic fever.

Heart valve damage is a serious and common complication of rheumatic fever leading to multiple problems in the future. In addition to the narrowing or leakage of the valve, heart rhythm abnormalities may occur.

Currently, because of the availability of antibiotics, this problem occurs less often. Early treatment with antibiotics

143

prevents the progression of pharyngitis or scarlet fever to rheumatic fever and rheumatic heart disease.

Can Anemia affect the heart?

Anemia refers to a reduction in the number of circulating red blood cells or a decrease in the *hemoglobin* (a measure of red blood cells concentration). Red blood cells carry oxygen to the various organs of the body. General presentation of anemia includes shortness of breath on exertion, fatigue, dizziness, and palpitations (the sensation of fast heartbeats) and a pale skin color.

There are a number of conditions that cause anemia, including blood loss, increased destruction of red blood cells or decreased production of red blood cells.

Heart conditions related to anemia include increased heart rate, which might occasionally lead to rhythm abnormalities. Because the heart is trying to compensate for the decreased ability of the blood to deliver oxygen to the organs, the workload of the heart increases, and this might lead to or worsen already existing heart failure.

Individuals with underlying coronary heart disease may experience increased frequency of chest pain that can occasionally result in a heart attack.

For individuals with heart failure, anemia almost doubles their chance of a poor outcome. Heart failure is worsened by anemia. Correcting anemia in these individuals might improve their survival and both the heart and kidney functions.

Can Ankylosing Spondylitis affect the heart?

Ankylosing spondylitis is a chronic condition caused by inflammation of the axial skeleton (back). This condition manifests by pain and stiffness of the spine. It usually affects adults. This disease also affects other organ systems, such as the heart, eyes, and lungs. It has been estimated that 50% of patients with ankylosing spondylitis have some sort of heart involvement.

Heart manifestations of this disease include *valvular heart disease* (disease of the heart valves), mainly affecting the *aortic valve*. This causes the valve to leak, which leads to increase in the workload on the heart. Also the mitral valve might be involved, which could result in *mitral valve prolapse*.

Individuals with this condition can also develop heart rhythm problems. Some of them might need a pacemaker.

What are the effects of Diabetes on the heart?

Diabetes is a common disease. There are two kinds of diabetes, Type 1 and Type 2. Type 1 is caused by lack of secretion of *insulin* from the pancreas. It usually occurs at young age. Type 2 occurs when the pancreas does not secrete enough insulin and there is resistance to the actions of insulin by the body. This form of diabetes usually affects adults.

Diabetes type 2 is of special importance because it is linked to obesity. Obese individuals have more than ten times the chance to develop diabetes than same-aged lean individuals.

Diabetes has also been linked to increased cholesterol levels, mainly LDL (bad cholesterol), increased triglycerides, and depressed HDL (good cholesterol). This, in turn, increases the risk for coronary heart disease.

Individuals with diabetes frequently have hypertension (high blood pressure). It is estimated that close to half of the individuals with diabetes have hypertension. The presence of hypertension in individuals with diabetes increases the risk for heart disease dramatically, even at levels regarded to be normal for other healthy individuals.

Individuals with diabetes have a higher risk to develop coronary heart disease because of elevated blood sugar and associated changes in blood cholesterol and blood pressure. In addition to heart disease, diabetics have an increase in blood clotting.

Diabetes is a strong risk factor for developing an enlarged heart and heart failure.

Good diabetes control and the control of other risk factors such as hypertension, increased cholesterol, and obesity are of great importance in decreasing the incidence and complications of heart disease in individuals with diabetes.

 **Chapter 14**

Cardiovascular Disease Prevention

Peter P. Toth, MD, PhD, FAAFP, FACC

Why is it important to learn about Coronary Heart Disease (CHD)?

Heart disease is the leading cause of death and disability for men and women in industrialized nations. Therefore, taking steps to prevent heart disease is extremely important. The economic and human cost of heart disease is staggering. In 2002, the cost of treating coronary heart disease (CHD) was over 112 billion dollars in the United States alone. Heart disease can also severely compromise not only the length but also the quality of life. The development of CHD greatly increases the risk of heart attack, sudden death, and congestive heart failure. Unfortunately, up to one-third of people who have their first heart attack die without prior warning. Although angioplasty and coronary artery bypass surgery have become routine procedures for helping to maintain blood flow to heart muscle, preventing heart disease is and will always form the cornerstone for preventing death and disability from CHD.

What causes heart attacks?

Heart attacks occur from progressive injury to the walls of the coronary arteries, blood vessels which nourish heart muscle. Coronary arterial injury begins at an early age. Many young men killed in the Korean and Vietnamese conflicts already had evidence of coronary disease at the age of 18 or 19 years. It is not uncommon for people to have heart attacks by the age of 35 or 40, especially if they have one or more risk factors for the development of CHD. Consequently, it stands to reason that, if we intervene early and aggressively, we may be able to retard or even prevent the development and progression of CHD. Studies have proven this to be true.

What are risk factors for developing CHD?

Over the course of the last five decades, great progress has been made in identifying many of the most important factors that predispose people to the development of CHD. We refer to these as "***risk factors***," and these include elevated blood cholesterol, elevated blood pressure (hypertension), diabetes, cigarette smoking, depression and social stress, obesity, and a family history of CHD. These risk factors, either alone or in combination, impart progressive injury to blood vessel walls. The injured portion of the blood vessel develops foci of fatty buildup known as ***atheromatous plaque***. These plaques grow in size and lead to obstructions or blockages along the lumen of the coronary vessel. As the severity of the obstruction increases, less and less blood can flow through to the heart muscle. This leads to an ***oxygen deficit*** within the heart muscle which can manifest itself as chest pain, pressure, or tightness (***angina pectoris***). A heart attack occurs when an atheromatous plaque suddenly ruptures. The ruptured plaque becomes covered with clotted blood, and this leads to sudden cessation of blood flow to the heart muscle. If the obstruction is not rapidly relieved by emergency angioplasty or a clot buster, the affected portion of heart muscle dies. If the affected area of heart muscle is large enough, this can result in sudden death. If the patient survives, a heart attack can leave one disabled because of inability to tolerate physical exertion or even executing the routine activities of daily living. Controlling the severity of CHD risk factors is critical to the prevention of heart disease and heart attack.

Why is cholesterol considered a risk factor for developing CHD?

Based on studies performed around the world in both men and women and in every racial and ethnic group yet evaluated, increased blood cholesterol levels are unequivocally associated with increased risk for CHD. Our body tissues naturally produce cholesterol. The liver and brain are particularly capable of synthesizing cholesterol. We also derive cholesterol from many of the foods that we eat. For some people, simple lifestyle modification measures such as a low-fat diet and increased exercise are enough to reduce circulating blood levels of cholesterol. Many other people require a combination of medication and lifestyle modification to reduce their blood levels of cholesterol. The National Cholesterol Education Program has clearly defined cholesterol goals for people of varying levels of risk for CHD. The higher the risk for CHD, the lower the level of desirable cholesterol.

What are the three types of cholesterol?

There are three forms of cholesterol, forms that can be conveniently labeled as "the good, the bad, and the ugly."

Why is HDL considered the "good" cholesterol?

The *good cholesterol* is *HDL*, or *"high-density lipoprotein cholesterol."* HDL is beneficial because it helps to mop up blood vessel walls. It actually removes excess cholesterol from arterial walls and delivers it back to the liver for intestinal disposal. The higher your level of HDL, the lower your risk for developing CHD. A desirable level of HDL in men is 40 or more, while for women it is 50 or more. When HDL falls below these thresholds, lifestyle modification and/or medication are warranted to reduce risk for CHD. Aerobic exercise, smoking cessation, weight loss, and reducing carbohydrate ingestion all help to raise HDL. Statins (Crestor, Zocor, Lipitor), fibrates (Tricor, Lopid), and niacin can all raise HDL effectively. The benefits of these medications far, far outweigh their risks. If you are diabetic, the TZD drugs such as Avandia and Actos can also be used to raise HDL. The use of any particular one of these medications depends upon a variety of factors which your physician must sort out. Therapy is always individualized to the needs of individual patients. An HDL level cannot be too high. When it comes to HDL, the higher the better. For every 1 mg/dL elevation in HDL, risk for CHD decreases by 3%.

Why is LDL considered the "bad" cholesterol?

The bad cholesterol is *LDL*, or *"low-density lipoprotein."* Generally speaking, when it comes to LDL, the lower the better. A variety of drugs can be used to decrease blood levels of LDL. By blocking cholesterol absorption from the gastrointestinal tract, LDL levels can be lowered. Such medications include Welchol and Zetia. The best drugs for decreasing LDL are the statins. Many studies conducted throughout the world in men and women have shown that the reduction of LDL with statins is associated with substantial reductions in risk for heart attack, stroke, sudden death, angina, and heart failure. The evidence supporting the use of statins in patients with high LDL is unequivocal. LDL is the type of cholesterol that builds up in blood vessel walls. It is toxic to blood vessels and compromises their normal function. As LDL builds up, obstructions to the flow of blood develop, ultimately leading to blockages, episodic chest pain, and heart attack. LDL is public enemy number one.

What is Lp(a) and why is it considered the "ugly" cholesterol?

The ugly cholesterol is *Lp(a)*, or *lipoprotein(a)*. Lp(a) is truly a bad actor. It is particularly toxic to blood vessels. Many people are simply genetically programmed to have high Lp(a). People are not routinely screened for the ugly cholesterol. If you are having your cholesterol checked, make sure the panel being done includes a test for Lp(a). If it is high, it is particularly important to drive down your LDL. We do not yet have any medications that specifically reduce Lp(a) effectively. If Lp(a) is a problem, your physician should try to reduce your LDL to less than 80 in an effort to compensate for the elevation in the ugly cholesterol.

What are triglycerides (blood fats)?

Triglycerides or *blood fats* are also important. Interestingly, high triglycerides appear to be an even more important risk factor in women than in men. Triglycerides should be kept to less than 150. High triglycerides can be reduced by decreasing the intake of fat and through increased exercise. Fish oils enriched with omega-3 fatty acids can be particularly effective at reducing blood triglyceride levels and are a type of health food alternative to other medications. The fibrates, statins, and niacin can also reduce blood levels of triglycerides. In some cases Xenical therapy may be warranted. Some people lack the molecular machinery to break down triglycerides in their blood with efficiency. Xenical blocks the absorption of fat from the diet and can lead to very substantial reductions in blood triglyceride levels. One potential side-effect of Xenical is the passage of oily stools which can be accompanied by urgency. If your triglycerides have been normal and you suddenly begin to experience a steady rise in their levels, you should be evaluated for possible new-onset diabetes or thyroid disease. Maintaining blood fats and the various forms of cholesterol in the normal range are critical to the prevention of CHD.

Why is high blood pressure considered a risk factor for developing CHD?

Elevations in blood pressure are an important source of chronic, recurrent injury to blood vessel walls. *High blood pressure* has also been shown to strongly predispose both men and women to CHD. Once blood pressure begins to creep above 120/80 mm Hg, risk escalates continuously. People with blood pressure that exceeds 140/90 warrant intervention with medication. Blood pressure should be reduced to 130/80 or less under optimal conditions. If you are diabetic and have kidney disease, your blood pressure should be less than 125/75 mm Hg. Lifestyle modification with weight loss, exercise, and salt restriction is an important means by which to control elevated blood pressure or hypertension. If you have hypertension it is also important to avoid drugs that can raise blood pressure, such as the pseudoephedrine in over-the-counter decongestants.

What types of treatment are available to treat high blood pressure?

Many drugs are available to treat hypertension. Your doctor has to weigh many aspects of your overall clinical picture in order to arrive at an appropriate choice of drug to reduce your blood pressure. ACE inhibitors, beta-blockers, calcium channel blockers, diuretics, and alpha-blockers are commonly used. The majority of patients require the combination of two or more of these drugs to achieve adequate control of blood pressure. The risk for hypertension increases continuously as we age. This is why it is important that your blood pressure be checked at least once or twice per year. The risk for death and disability from cardiovascular disease doubles for every 20/10 mm Hg elevation in blood pressure. If your doctor wants to treat your blood pressure or add more types of medication to do it, be cooperative since hypertension dramatically increases risk for heart attack, stroke, sudden death, kidney disease, and blindness.

Only about 30% of patients reach their blood pressure goals. It is critically important that all patients form therapeutic alliances with their physicians and help to ensure that their blood pressure is lowered to appropriate levels. It is a good idea to invest in the purchase of a blood pressure measuring cuff and measure your blood pressure regularly. If it is creeping up, it is time to talk to your doctor. By the age of fifty, approximately 30% of white men and 50% of black men have hypertension. The percentages are similar for white and black women. If you have *isolated systolic hypertension* (the upper number is above 140 but the lower number is "normal" at less than 90), you warrant therapy. Isolated systolic hypertension is particularly dangerous and greatly magnifies risk for CHD and stroke. We no longer believe that increased blood pressure in the elderly helps to preserve blood flow to critical organs. High blood pressure is bad for everyone.

What is the relationship between diabetes and CHD?

The prevalence of diabetes is growing at an alarming rate. This is a worldwide problem. By the year 2025, the World Health Organization estimates that there will be 340 million diabetics throughout the world. The rising prevalence of obesity and sedentary lifestyle are largely to blame for this epidemic of diabetes. Diabetes is a vicious disease. It quadruples the risk for CHD and stroke and increases the risk for kidney failure, adult-onset blindness, and lower limb amputation about 10-fold. If you have diabetes, studies have shown that it is safe to assume that you have CHD. Consequently, your risk factors must be managed extremely aggressively.

There are well-defined thresholds for the management of risk factors in diabetics. Your blood sugars before breakfast and supper should be less than 120. It is best to keep your hemoglobin A1c (a measure of blood sugar control over a three-month period) at 6.5 or less. Blood pressure should be less than 130/80 in the absence of *kidney disease* (*diabetic nephropathy*). However, if a patient has developed kidney damage from chronic diabetes, then blood pressure should be less than 125/75. Your urine should be checked every year for evidence of kidney damage. This typically manifests itself as a protein leak. A rising serum creatinine level (a measure of kidney filtration capacity) also warrants further evaluation. Make sure your eyes are checked every year by an ophthalmologist so that the earliest signs of eye and retina damage can be detected and appropriately treated. Your LDL should be less than 100, triglycerides less than 150, and your HDL should be greater than 40 in a man and greater than 50 in a woman.

What are the symptoms of heart disease in a person with diabetes?

Heart disease in a diabetic can be tricky to detect. Because of damage to the nerves of the heart, diabetics may not experience classical warning signs of heart attack. Diabetics may have severe CHD and never experience chest pain. Consequently, if you are diabetic, if you are developing shortness of breath, lightheadedness, pain in between your shoulder blades, or easily induced fatigue with minimal exertion, it is time to see you doctor for a heart evaluation.

Why is smoking considered a risk factor for developing CHD?

Smoking is extremely detrimental to your heart and blood vessels. Smoking accelerates the aging of your entire cardiovascular system. Women who develop CHD in their late thirties or early forties are almost always smokers. Although smoking greatly increases the risk for lung cancer, it actually increases the risk for CHD even more. If you smoke, it is critical that you quit. Ninety percent of the battle to quit smoking is between your ears. If you want to quit smoking, you will. If you are half-hearted about smoking cessation, odds are you will fail.

Pharmacologic aids for smoking cessation are available. Nicorette gum and nicotine patches (Habitrol, Nicotrol) help provide the nicotine necessary to prevent symptoms of withdrawal. It is important to wean yourself from nicotine. If you use the patch, start at 21 mg per day for one month, then go to 14 mg per day for one month, and then 7 mg per day for one month, and then stop. Zyban is a pill that helps to reduce the intensity of nicotine withdrawal. When taken at 150 mg twice daily, patients should decrease their cigarette consumption by one cigarette every other day until they quit. This way they reduce consumption at a slow but sustainable pace and limit the intensity of withdrawal. Some people simply have to go "cold turkey." The effort required to quit smoking is always worth it.

What is the connection between Hormone Replacement Therapy (HRT) and CHD?

For many years it was believed that estrogen replacement therapy would decrease risk for CHD. After all, during the premenopausal years women are highly protected from the development of CHD. Unfortunately, this has not turned out to be the case. ***Hormone replacement therapy (HRT)*** for post-menopausal women without CHD appears to slightly increase the risk for heart attack. Consequently, if a woman has low risk for CHD, then the use of HRT may be largely an issue of quality of life. If she is having severe hot flashes and night sweats, pain with intercourse, or mood swings, then a 3- to 5-year course of HRT is a reasonable choice to help her get through menopause. Where the issue appears to be particularly important is in women who have established CHD. Women with CHD should not take hormone replacement therapy as multiple studies have shown that HRT significantly increases risk for heart attack in the face of established coronary artery disease.

Is alcohol considered a risk factor for CHD or can it be healthful?

Alcohol consumption is generally discussed in negative terms by both health care providers and the press because of the risk for alcoholism. However, when consumed in moderation, wine (2-8 ounces daily) can promote health, not compromise it. Increased wine consumption appears to underlie the so-called French paradox: the people in France eat some of the richest food on earth, yet their risk for CHD is the lowest in the Western hemisphere. Similar findings apply to the people living in Italy.

Wine increases the levels of HDL in your blood. It does this by two mechanisms. First, it stimulates increased production of HDL by the liver. Second, alcohol helps to decrease the breakdown and clearance of HDL in your blood. Red wine appears to be particularly beneficial. If it has been stored and matured in oak barrels it tends to contain high concentrations of potent, naturally occurring antioxidants such as quercetin, catechin, and reservatrol. These antioxidants are protective to the cardiovascular system. But, remember, all things in moderation!

What is the relationship between antioxidant vitamins and CHD?

For a number of years people have been encouraged to consume mega-doses of such antioxidant vitamins as vitamins E and C and beta-carotene. Images of Linus Pauling scooping tablespoons of vitamin C into his orange juice have endured. Although Dr. Pauling won the Nobel prize twice, when it comes to antioxidant supplements in the gel capsule or the big white pills, he was wrong.

In both the Heart Outcomes Protection and Evaluation Study and the Heart Protection Study, antioxidant vitamin supplements provided absolutely no protection from the development of CHD, heart attack, stroke, or other bad cardiovascular outcomes. In fact, in another study known as the HDL Atherosclerosis Treatment Study, the addition of antioxidant vitamins to patients receiving statins and niacin dramatically blunts the ability of these drugs to raise HDL and decrease risk for adverse cardiovascular outcomes. It is no longer recommended that patients take antioxidant supplements such as vitamins E and C.

Should I take an aspirin a day to prevent a heart attack?

Aspirin has been shown to reduce heart attacks in high-risk patients such as those with established coronary artery disease, peripheral vascular disease or strokes. Also, diabetics are considered high-risk patients. We advise one aspirin a day to all diabetics with or without history of coronary disease. Healthy males over the age of 40 and females over the age of 50 are advised to take an aspirin a day to reduce the chance of a first heart attack. This recommendation is not universally adopted and should be weighed against the risks of aspirin, mainly ulcer disease. Some data suggest that patients with normal hs-CRP (a blood test that measures the degree of inflammation in the body) can be used as a guide to whether we should treat healthy people with an aspirin. Patients with abnormally elevated hs-CRP might benefit from one aspirin a day. The current recommended dose of aspirin is 81 mg (baby aspirin) for heart attack prevention.

In conclusion . . . .

Cardiovascular disease is preventable! Identifying and treating risk factors which predispose people to the development of heart and vascular disease is tantamount to living not only longer, but also more productively and free of disability. Risk factors can be improved through both lifestyle modification and medication. If you require medication to treat cholesterol, blood pressure, or diabetes, do not consider this a failure. Be glad that we have the therapeutic means at our disposal to help address these problems. If multiple medications are required, take this in stride and understand that tight control of all risk factors unequivocally affects your risk for heart and vascular disease, the No. 1 cause of death and disability in both men and women in industrialized nations throughout the world.

 ***Chapter 15***

Medications for Cardiovascular Disorders

Nidal Harb, MD, FACC, FACP

Since 1919, cardiovascular diseases have been the No.1 killer in the United States, responsible for more than 40% of American deaths. Worldwide, more than half of the population suffers from complications of *atherosclerosis*, or hardening of the arteries.

Over the past 25 years, there has been a tremendous progress in the development of new procedures and techniques to treat cardiovascular diseases.

One of the major advances has been the development of newer cardiac medications. In this chapter, we will discuss information about medications which are used to treat many aspects of heart disease.

This chapter will provide you with useful information about medications which you may be taking, as well as potential alternatives. Certainly, this book is not intended to tell you which, if any, medication is best for you since this only can be determined by your physician after appropriate evaluation.

What types of health conditions will be discussed in this chapter?

In this chapter, we will be discussing medications for treatment of heart failure, high blood pressure, lipid-lowering medications, arrhythmia disorder, coronary artery disease, and heart attacks, in addition to other vascular problems, including erectile dysfunction.

How do "heart medications" work?

These medications usually have two names: the *brand name*, which may differ from one company to another depending on the pharmaceutical manufacturer; and the *generic name*, which refers to all medications with the same chemical structure.

In the USA, due to Food and Drug Administration (FDA) regulations, the brand and generic names should be equal in effectiveness and safety. Sometimes, the tablets may differ in size or color due to the inactive substance which is usually added to the medications. Your physician may allow the use of generic medications; however, please keep in mind that not all brand names can be obtained generically because of the patent protection law in the USA.

Once medication is taken it is absorbed in the stomach or gut, processed in the liver and eventually eliminated from the body either through the kidney or through the liver. In order to obtain a certain level of medication in the body, the drug has to be taken on a certain schedule, depending on the medications used. Some medications have a special delivery system which makes them long-acting.

161

In many situations, medications may be used for several different medical problems. Your doctor will individualize your treatment based on your specific problems.

How do antihypertensive medications help to reduce high blood pressure?

Over the past 50 years there has been a significant drop in the incidence of heart attacks and strokes. One of the main reasons for this drop is the development of newer ***antihypertensive medications*** to treat high blood pressure.

Nowadays, there are more than 100 different medications which could be used to treat this ailment. There is also a combination of different drugs which could be utilized. The most commonly used antihypertensive drugs are:

1)   Diuretic drugs
2)   Beta-blockers
3)   Calcium channel blockers
4)   ACE inhibitors
5)   Alpha blockers
6)   Angiotensin II blockers (ARB)
7)   Centrally acting drugs
8)   Other antihypertensive medications

Beta-blockers, ACE inhibitors, ARBs, and calcium channel blockers, in addition to diuretics, are the most commonly used medications. Less frequently, alpha-blockers, centrally acting drugs such as hydralazine and minoxidil are used in addition to other drugs.

Most antihypertensive medications reduce high blood pressure by relaxing the vessel wall, thus increasing the diameter of the vessel. Others may reduce the force with which the heart pumps the blood. Diuretics will cause increased urine outputs, which will result in reduced volume of blood present in the circulation.

BLOOD PRESSURE MEASUREMENT TECHNIQUES

METHOD	NOTES
In-office	Two readings, 5 minutes apart, sitting in chair. Confirm elevated reading in contralateral arm.
Ambulatory BP monitoring	Indicated for evaluation of "white coat hypertension." Absence of 10-20 percent BP decrease during sleep may indicate increased CVD risk.
Patient self-check	Provides information on response to therapy. May help improve adherence to therapy and is useful for evaluating "white coat hypertension."

CLASSIFICATION OF BLOOD PRESSURE (BP)

Category	SBP mmHg		DBP mmHg
Normal	<120	and	<80
Prehypertension	120-139	or	80-89
Hypertension, stage I	140-159	or	90-99
Hypertension, stage 2	$\geq$160	or	$\geq$100

SBP = Systolic blood pressure
DBP = Diastolic blood pressure

PRINCIPLES OF LIFESTYLE MODIFICATION
- ♥ Encourage healthy lifestyles for all individuals
- ♥ Prescribe lifestyle modifications for all patients with prehypertension and hypertension.
- ♥ Components of lifestyle modifications include weight reduction, DASH eating plan, dietary sodium restriction, aerobic physical activity, and moderation of alcohol consumption.

LIFESTYLE MODIFICATION RECOMMENDATIONS

Modification	Recommendation	Avg SBP Reduction [†]
Weight Reduction	Maintain normal body weight (body mass index 18.5-24.9 kg/m^2)	5-20 mmHg/10 kg
DASH eating plan	Adopt a diet rich in fruits, vegetables, and low-fat dairy products with reduced content of saturated and total fat.	8-14 mmHg
Dietary sodium reduction	Reduce dietary sodium intake to $\leq$ 100 mmol per day (2.4 g sodium or 6 g sodium chloride)	2-8 mmHg
Aerobic physical activity	Regular aerobic physical activity (e.g., brisk walking) at least 30 minutes per day, most days of the week	4-9 mmHg
Moderation of alcohol consumption	Men: Limit to $\leq$2 drinks* per day. Women and lighter weight persons: Limit to $\leq$1 drink* per day	2-4 mmHg

[†] 1 drink = ½ oz or 15 mL ethanol   (e.g., 12 oz beer, 5 oz wine, 1.5 oz   80-proof whiskey).

MEDICATIONS FOR HIGH BLOOD PRESSURE

TABLE A

MEDICATION AND ACTION	GENERIC NAME	EXAMPLES OF BRAND NAMES	USES	HOW TAKEN	SPECIFIC SIDE EFFECTS	SPECIFIC PRECAUTIONS
CENTRALLY ACTING AGENTS These medications affect control centers in the brain that decrease blood pressure	Methyldopa Guanfacine Guanabenz Clonidine	*Aldomet* *Tenex* *Wytensin* *Catapres*	Decrease blood pressure	Swallow tablet at prescribed dose and schedule	Fluid retention (edema) Fever Insomnia Lower blood pressure Dizziness Liver function or blood cell count abnormalities Dry mouth	May need to stand slowly from lying position to avoid sudden blood pressure drop and faintness. Do not stop taking abruptly
	Clonidine (skin patch)	*Catapres-TTS*		Apply skin patch at prescribed schedule	Drowsiness Itching (skin patch)	Double-check possibility of interactions with other medication
DIRECT ACTING VASODILATORS These medications cause the muscle in the walls of blood vessels to relax	Hydralazine	*Apresoline*	Decrease blood pressure Reduce work load of heart	Swallow tablet at prescribed dose and schedule	Low blood pressure Dizziness Lupus syndrome (blisters, chest pain, joint pain, weakness) Diarrhea Headache	May need to stand slowly from lying position to avoid sudden blood pressure drop and faintness.
	Minoxidil	*Loniten*	Decrease blood pressure	Swallow tablet at prescribed dose and schedule	Fast heartbeat Flushing Fluid retention (edema) Excessive hair growth	Check resting heart rate periodically. Check weight (to assess fluid gain)
PERIPHERALLY ACTING AGENTS These medications exert their effects on the nerves of the body that are involved in blood pressure regulation	Guadadrel Guanethidine Mecamylamine Prazosin Rauwolfia Alkaloids Terazosin Doxazosin	*Hylorel* *Ismelin* *Inversine* *Minipress* *Harmonyl* *Raudixin* *Rauzide* *Serpasil* *Hytrin* *Cardura*	Decrease blood pressure	Swallow tablet or capsule at prescribed dose and schedule	Fluid retention (edema) Low blood pressure Dizziness Drowsiness Difficulty ejaculating Mental depression Stomach and bowel disturbances	Double-check possibility of interactions with medications. May need to stand slowly from lying position to avoid sudden blood pressure drop and faintness

Beta blockers *(see Table F)* Calcium blockers *(see Table G)* Diuretics *(see Table C)* Angiotension converting enzyme {ACE} inhibitors *(see Table C)*

This list is not comprehensive and does not represent an endorsement of any product listed.

How are antiarrhythmic medications used to treat abnormal heart rhythm and rate?

These drugs are used to treat abnormal heart rhythm and rate. The most commonly used medications are:

1) Beta-blocker
2) Calcium channel blockers
3) Digitalis
4) Other anti-arrhythmic medications

Arrhythmias are abnormalities of the heart rhythm which occur when there is a disruption in the normal cardiac rhythm. This could be due to abnormalities in the atrium, which is the upper chamber of the heart or in the ventricles, which are the lower chambers of the heart.

These groups of drugs are given to regulate the heartbeats and/or to prevent the arrhythmias from occurring.

These medications can be given intravenously and/or orally, depending on the clinical situation and the availability of these drugs. The appropriate medication will be selected based on the form of arrhythmia you have. Unfortunately, these drugs have potential side effects, such as slowing of the heartbeat, worsening of the arrhythmias, reduction of blood pressure, and other symptoms which will be listed in the graphics.

MEDICATIONS FOR RHYTHM DISORDERS
TABLE B

Medication and Action	Generic Name	Examples of Brand Names	Uses	How Taken	Specific Side Effects	Specific Precautions
Antiarrhythmic Agents Medications for fast or irregular heartbeats – alter the way in which electrical currents flow through the conduction system and heart muscle. The change in the electrical characteristics of the heart may reduce the ability of a heart rhythm abnormality to begin or continue	Quinidine	*Cardioquin* *Cin-Quin* *Duraquin* *Quinaglute* *Quinalan* *Quinidex* *Quinora*	Help control various rhythm disorders	Swallow pill at prescribed dose and schedule.	Diarrhea Dizziness Stomach upset Ringing in ears Passing out	Avoid if known sensitivity to quinine. Digoxin dose will need to be adjusted because quinidine causes digoxin levels in blood to rise
	Procainamide (tablet, capsule, intravenous)	*Procan SR* *Pronestyl* *Pronestyl-SR*		Oral	Lupus syndrome (blisters, chest pain, joint pain, weakness)	Avoid if known sensitivity to procaine
	Disopyramide	*Norpace* *Norpace CR*		Oral	Blurry Vision Urinary obstruction (men) Dry mouth Congestive heart failure	Elderly patients may be more prone to side effects. Caution if milk sensitivity – tablets contain lactose (milk sugar)
	Lidocaine (intravenous)	*Xylocaine*		Injection	Confusion Seizures	
	Phenytoin	*Dilantin*		Oral/injection	Overgrowth of gums Drowsiness	
	Mexiletine	*Mexitil*			Stomach upset Trembling, unsteadiness	
	Tocainide	*Tonocard*			Stomach upset Trembling, unsteadiness Blood cell abnormalities	
	Flecainide	*Tambocor*			Congestive heart failure Dizziness, visual disturbance	Avoid after recent heart attack
	Moricizine	*Ethmozine*			Stomach upset Dizziness, headache	

TABLE B. *(continued)*

Medication and Action	Generic Name	Examples of Brand Names	Uses	How Taken	Specific Side Effects	Specific Precautions
	Bretylium (intravenous)	*Bretylol*			Low blood pressure	
Antiarrhythmic agents continued Medications for slow heartbeats – act by affecting the nervous system's control of heart rate	Amiodarone	*Cordarone*	Help control various rhythm disorders	Orally or injected into vein	Bluish skin discoloration Overactive or underactive thyroid Lung scarring (fibrosis) Nerve damage Spots in corneas of eyes Liver abnormalities Stomach upset	Digoxin dose will need to be adjusted because amiodarone causes digoxin levels in blood to rise. Periodically have blood tests and chest x-ray, pulmonary function tests and eye examination
	Adenosine	*Adenocard*	For rapid treatment of fast heartbeats originating from the upper parts of the heart (atria and antrioventricular node)	Rapidly injected into a vein	Chest heaviness Flushing Nausea Headache Shortness of breath/ asthma Slow heartbeat Dizziness (All side effects are very brief)	Very short-acting medication. Effects enhanced by dipyridamole. Effects reduced by caffeine and certain
	Ibutilide	*Corvert*		Rapidly injected into a vein		Asthma medications (theophyllines)
	Atropine (intravenous)		For temporary acceleration of certain slow heartbeats	Administered by vein	Rapid heartbeat Mouth dryness Blurred vision Difficulty urinating	Avoid in glaucoma, urinary obstruction
	Isoproterenol (intravenous)	*Isuprel*	For temporary acceleration of certain slow heartbeats	Administered by vein	Rapid heartbeat Blood pressure swings	Avoid in angina

Beta blockers (*see Table F*) Calcium channel blockers (*see Table G*)
This list is not comprehensive and does not represent an endorsement of any product listed.

Which types of medications can combat heart failure?

Although some manifestations of heart disease seem to be waning, heart failure has become an epidemic. The death rates from stroke and myocardial infarction dropped substantially with the advances in medications and intervention; however, the number of patients with significant ventricular dysfunction or pump failure continues to rise.

Heart failure is not a disease, per se, but rather it is a result of an injury, which can produce muscle weakness resulting in pump failure or stiffness of the muscle. The most common cause of the injury is a heart attack due to coronary artery disease, an infectious process like virus, hypertension or valve dysfunction. Other causes will be discussed in greater detail in a separate chapter.

Treatment for heart failure involves, first, treating the *cause* of the heart failure itself, and second, treating the *symptoms* of heart failure.

The non-pharmacological approach to the treatment – such as a low-salt diet, weight restrictions, patient's education on activity and medications – is certainly recommended. However, in most patients, this is not enough, and many will require medications, as well. After evaluating the severity of heart failure, the medications which are most commonly used are diuretics, angiotensin-converting enzyme (ACE) inhibitors, beta-adrenergic blockers, angiotensin receptor blockers (ARB), aldosterone antagonists and digoxin. For details, please see Table C.

MEDICATIONS FOR HEART FAILURE
TABLE C

Medication and Action	Generic Name	Example of Brand Names	Uses	How Taken	Specific side effects	Specific precautions
Angiotensin converting enzyme inhibitors (ACE Inhibitors) These medications dilate arteries and decrease resistance to the flow of blood being pumped from the heart. The result is lower blood pressure and easier pumping for the heart	Captopril Moexipril Enalapril Lisinopril Quinapril Benazepril Fosinopril Ramipril Trandolapril Perindopril	*Capoten Univasc Vasotec Zestril/Prinivil Accupril Lotensin Monopril Altace Mavik Aceon*	Decreased blood pressure Reduce workload of heart	Swallow tablet at prescribed dose and schedule	Low blood pressure Rash Elevated potassium Persistent dry cough Abnormal sense of taste Stomach upset Swelling of the skin	Use with caution when taking simultaneously with potassium sparing diuretics (below) and patients with kidney problems
Diuretics	Chlorthalidone Chlorothiazide Hydrochlorothiazide Methyclothiazide Metolazone	*Hygroton Thalitone Diuril Esidrix HydroDIURIL Oretic Aquatensen Enduron Diulo Zaroxolyn*	Milder diuretics for: Decreasing blood pressure Gentle fluid reduction	Swallow tablet at prescribed dose and schedule	Low potassium High calcium Low sodium Elevated blood glucose (sugar) Risk of gout Stomach upset Pancreatitis	Check potassium, sodium, calcium, glucose and creatinine periodically
	Amiloride Spironolactone Triamterene Bendroflumethiazide Benzthiazide Indapamide Quinethazone Polythiazide Trichlormethiazide Hydroflumethiazide	*Midamor Aldactone Dyrenium*	As above, but without loss of potassium in the urine ("potassium-sparing")	Swallow tablet at prescribed dose and schedule	Male breast enlargement (with spironolactone) Elevated potassium Stomach upset	Check potassium, sodium, calcium, glucose periodically.

TABLE C. *(Continued)*

Medication and Action	Generic Name	Example of Brand Names	Uses	How Taken	Specific side effects	Specific precautions
Diuretics *(continued)*	Bumetanide Ethacrynic acid Furosemide (tablet or intravenous) Torsemide Nesiritide	*Bumex* *Edecrin* *Lasix* *Demadex* *Natrecor*	Potent diuretics for vigorous reduction of excess fluid Intravenous drip	Swallow tablet at prescribed dose schedule. Administer by vein	Excess fluid output Low blood pressure Low potassium Low sodium Elevated blood glucose (sugar) Risk of gout Stomach upset Decreased hearing Muscle cramps	Double-check possibility of interactions with other medications. Check potassium, sodium, calcium, and glucose periodically
Inotropic Agents These medications increase the squeezing strength of the heart muscle. The effect is to increase the amount of blood the heart is able to pump through the circulation	Digitalis Digoxin Digitoxin Digoxin (intravenous)	*Lanoxin* *Lanoxicaps* *Crystodigin* *Lanoxin*	Increase pumping strength of heart Help control certain rhythm disorders	Swallow tablet at prescribed dose and schedule. Administer by vein	Stomach upset Loss of appetite Visual disturbance Slow or irregular heartbeat	Avoid low potassium level; promotes side effects. Check for drug interactions, particularly drugs that can cause digitalis level to become too high, especially verapamil, amiodarone and quinidine
	Dopamine (intravenous) Dobutamine (intravenous) Amrinone (intravenous)	*Intropin* *Dobutrex* *Inocor*	Increase pumping strength of heart	Administer by vein	Rhythm disturbances Nausea Headache Chest pain Cold hands and feet	

Nitrates *(see Table E)* **Direct-acting vasodilators** *(see Table A)*
This list is not comprehensive and does not represent an endorsement of any product listed.

How do lipid-lowering medications address coronary artery disease?

It has been clearly established, and without any doubt, that there is a direct link between the development of coronary artery disease or plugged arteries and cholesterol/ triglyceride levels. Over the past few years, physicians have been more aggressive in lowering cholesterol and triglyceride levels. The National Cholesterol Education Program has issued guidelines for physicians and patients to follow. A summary of the guidelines is shown here.

MAJOR RISK FACTORS (EXCLUSIVE OF LDL CHOLESTEROL)

Cigarette smoking

Hypertension (BLOOD PRESSURE ≥140/90 mmHg or on antihypertensive medication)

Low HDL cholesterol (<40 mg/dL)*

Family history of premature CHD (CHD in male first degree relative <55 years; CHD in female first degree relative <65 years).

Age (men >45 years; women ≥55 years)

*HDL cholesterol ≥60 mg/dL counts as "negative" risk factor; its presence removes one risk factor from the total count

---

LDL CHOLESTEROL – PRIMARY TARGET OF THERAPY

70-99	Optimal
100-129	Near optimal/above optimal
130-159	Borderline high
160-189	High
$\geq$190	Very high

TOTAL CHOLESTEROL

<200	Desirable
200-239	Borderline high
$\geq$240	High

HDL CHOLESTEROL

<40	Low
$\geq$60	High

CLASSIFICATION OF SERUM TRIGLYCERIDES (MG/DL)

<150	Normal
150-199	Borderline high
200-499	High
$\geq$500	Very High

The advancement in technology also has allowed for the development of numerous medications to treat hyperlipidemia.

LIPID-LOWERING MEDICATIONS
TABLE D

Medication and Action	Generic Name	Examples of Brand Names	Uses	How Taken	Specific Side Effects	Specific Precautions
Bile acid sequestrants These medications chemically bind to bile acids in the intestine. Bile acids are made by the body from cholesterol. They normally pass from the liver into the intestine but a portion returns into the bloodstream through the intestinal wall. These medications do not permit them to return so more cholesterol is used to make more bile acids, which in turn are also excreted. Eventually, the body's pool of cholesterol decreases.	Cholestyramine	*Questran (powder)* *Prevalite (powder)*	Lower cholesterol	Mix powder with 4-6 ounces beverage (it will not actually dissolve) and drink all the liquid. Mix with other liquid foods if desired (soup, cereal, fruit) Eat it like a candy bar - chew thoroughly	Constipation Abdominal pain and upset	Avoid taking at same time as other medications Take other medications 1 hour before or 6 hours after taking this medication. Double-check possibility of interactions with other medications
	Colesevelam	*WelChol*		Tablets orally		
	Colestipol	*Colestid (granules)*	Lower cholesterol	Mix powder with beverage (4 to 6 ounces) – it will not actually dissolve – and drink all the liquid. Mix with other liquid foods if desired (soup, cereal, fruit)	Constipation Abdominal pain and upset	Other cardiovascular medications that may be affected: digitalis, anticoagulants, propranolol, thiazide, diuretics. Do not take as dry powder
Gemfibrozil This medication reduces triglycerides and VLDL cholesterol and raises HDL cholesterol. The way it does this is not well understood.	Gemfibrozil	*Lopid*	Lower triglycerides Raise HDL cholesterol	Swallow tablet at prescribed dose and schedule	Stomach upset Nausea, diarrhea Rash Muscle pain, weakness Liver function problems Dizziness Blurred vision	Avoid statins while taking this medication. The risk of muscle inflammation increases

TABLE D (continued)

Medication and Action	Generic Name	Examples of Brand Names	Uses	How Taken	Specific Side Effects	Specific Precautions
HMG-CoA reductase inhibitor This medication enhances your body's ability to rid itself of cholesterol	Lovastatin Pravastatin Simvastatin Atorvastatin Fluvastatin Rosuvastatin	*Mevacor* *Pravachol* *Zocor* *Lipitor* *Lescol* *Crestor*	Lower LDL cholesterol Lower triglycerides Raise HDL cholesterol (slightly)	Swallow tablet at prescribed dose and schedule	Blurred vision Muscle pain, weakness Stomach upset Liver function problems Insomnia Headache	Do not take gemfibrozil or nicotinic acid (niacin) while taking this medication unless prescribed by a physician. The risk of muscle inflammation increased. Other medications that may interact include cyclosporine, other immuno-suppressants, warfarin, clofibrate. Blood tests for liver function should be performed periodically, at least for the first year
Bile acid sequestrants (Continued) **Niacin** (nicotinic acid) This medication reduces your body's ability to manufacture VLDL cholesterol	Niacin	*Nia-Bid* *Niacels* *Nicobid* *Nicolar* *Slo-Niacin* *Nicotinex (elixir)* *Niacin SR*	Lower LDL cholesterol Lower triglycerides Raise HDL cholesterol	Swallow tablet (or elixir) at prescribed dose and schedule. Do not break or crush long-acting forms	Flushing, warm feeling Headache Stomach upset Liver function problem Itching	Side effects can be minimized by starting at low doses, taking with food, and building up to recommended dose . Flushing may decrease by taking aspirin before dose
Fenofibrate	Fenofibrate	*Tricor*	Lower triglycerides	Swallow capsule at prescribed dose and schedule	Stomach upset Rash	Persistent flushing can be reduced by taking 1 aspirin one-half hour before dose. Blood tests for liver function should be performed occasionally
Clofibrate This medication reduces triglycerides and, to a lesser extent, cholesterol (when triglycerides are also high), but the way it works is not understood	Clofibrate	*Atromid-S*	Lower triglycerides Lower cholesterol	Swallow capsule at prescribed dose and schedule	Gallstones Kidney problems Stomach upset Muscle pain, weakness Pancreatitis Liver function problems	Periodic blood tests for liver function, muscle inflammation (creatine kinase) and blood count are advisable
Dextrothyroxine This medication increases your body's ability to break down and remove cholesterol, but the mechanism is unclear	Dextrothyroxine	*Choloxin*	Lower cholesterol	Swallow tablet at prescribed dose and schedule	Heart attack Angina Hyperactive thyroid	Can interact with other medications, especially digitalis and anticoagulants

Dietary measures should be attempted first except in severe cases. Continue to follow dietary recommendations while taking medications. For all medications, lipid values should be checked within 3 months to determine the degree of success and to decide whether a change in dose or medication is needed. This list is not comprehensive and does not represent an endorsement of any product listed.

Which types of medications are effective for treatment of Coronary Artery Disease?

Coronary artery disease, or plugged arteries, is the leading cause of death in the United States and also worldwide. This disease is manifested by symptoms of chest pains (or angina pectoris), by a condition called unstable angina, by a heart attack, or by cardiac arrest.

Treatment for this serious condition could be pharmacological or interventional. In this chapter we will be discussing only the pharmacological approach. Medications may include nitrates, beta-blockers, calcium channel blockers, thrombolytics, and antiplatelet agents.

Nitrates

♥ **General side effects:** Headache, dizziness, lightheadedness, fast pulse, nausea.

♥ **General Precautions:** After chewing chewable tablets, hold in your mouth for 2 minutes before swallowing.

♥Alcohol may worsen some side effects (dizziness, lightheadedness).

♥ Some side effects (headache) generally lessen after several days of taking the medication.

♥ A rebound effect (sudden worsening of angina or a heart attack) may occur if nitrate use is suddenly stopped. A tapered withdrawal is recommended.

♥ The effect of nitrates diminishes if a constant amount is in the bloodstream all the time ("tolerance").

♥ Skin patches should be removed for a period of time each day.

MEDICATIONS FOR ANGINA PECTORIS: NITRATES
TABLE E

Medication and Action	Generic Name	Examples of Brand Names	Uses	How Taken	Specific Precautions
Nitrates The nitrates all have the following actions: 1) Dilate veins of the body 2) Dilate arteries of the body 3) Dilate coronary arteries	Nitroglycerin	*Nitrostat* (tablets)	Shorten angina attack Prevent anticipated angina attack	Let tablet dissolve under tongue at onset of angina, while sitting. If needed, repeat dose twice, 5 minutes between doses. One tablet under tongue at onset of activity predicted to cause angina	Loses potency 3-6 months after container is opened. Remove cotton plug and leave out. Keep container tightly closed. If angina persists for 15 minutes, go to doctor or emergency room
The effects of these actions are: 1) Redistribution of some of the volume of blood from the chambers of your heart to the veins of the body. This decreases the amount of stretching of the heart muscle. The less stretch or stress, the less oxygen the heart uses. This is the main way that nitrates lower the heart's demand for oxygen, which is helpful in view of the reduced supply		*Nitrolingual* (spray)	Shorten angina attack Prevent anticipated angina attack	1 or 2 sprays on or under tongue at onset of angina, while sitting. If needed, repeat dose twice, 5 minutes between doses 1 or 2 sprays on or under tongue at onset of activity expected to cause angina	Do not shake container. Do not inhale. If angina persists for 15 minutes, go to doctor or emergency room
2) Lowering the resistance the heart encounters in pumping blood into the arteries. This decreases the work load of the heart so that its need for oxygen is reduced		*Nitrogard* (buccal {Extended release} tablets)	Prevent angina attacks	Place tablet between upper lip and gum or between cheek and gum. Allow to dissolve over 3-5 hours	Do not chew or swallow
3) Increase the amount of blood that can flow through partially blocked coronary arteries. This enhances the oxygen supply to the heart muscle		*Nitrol* (ointment) *Nitro-Bid* (ointment)	Prevent angina attacks	Spread (do not rub in) the prescribed amount of ointment in thin layer on hairless area of skin at prescribed schedule. Use applicator paper that is provided.	Clean off previous ointment before reapplying. Rotate application sites to avoid irritation

177

MEDICATIONS FOR ANGINA PECTORIS: NITRATES
TABLE E (continued)

Medication and Action	Generic Name	Examples of Brand Names	Uses	How Taken	Specific Precautions
Nitrates *(continued)*		Nitroglycerin-B.i.d. (capsules) *Minitran* *Nitrodisc* *Nitro-Dur* *Transderm-Nitro* *Deponit* (transdermal patches) *Nitro-B.i.d. IV* *Nitrol IV* *Nitrostat IV*	Prevent angina attacks	Swallow tablet at prescribed dose and schedule. Apply skin patch for prescribed duration on hairless skin	Do not stop taking abruptly (to avoid rebound). Rotate application sites to avoid irritation. Avoid skin with nicks or cuts. Remove patch for 6-8 hours before replacing (to avoid tolerance)
	Nitroglycerin (intravenous)	*Tridil*	Manage angina attack	Given by vein	
	Isosorbide dinitrate Isosorbide mononitrate	*Isordil (tablets)* *Sorbitrate (tablets)* *Dilatrate (tablets)* *Imdur* *Ismo* *Monoket*	Prevent angina attacks	Swallow tablet or capsule at prescribed schedule with full glass of water on empty stomach	Do not stop taking abruptly (to avoid rebound)
	Pentaerythritol	*Peritrate (tablets)*	Prevent angina attack	Swallow tablet at prescribed schedule with full glass of water on an empty stomach	Do not stop taking abruptly (to avoid rebound)
	Erythritol tetranitrate	*Cardilate (tablets)*	Prevent angina attacks	Swallow tablet at prescribed schedule with full glass of water on empty stomach	Do not stop taking abruptly (to avoid rebound)

This list is not comprehensive and does not represent an endorsement of any product listed.

MEDICATIONS FOR ANGINA PECTORIS: BETA-BLOCKERS
TABLE F

Medication and Action Beta-blockers	Generic Name	Examples of Brand Names	Uses	How Taken	Specific Side Effects	Specific Precautions
The beta-blockers all have the following actions: 1) Slow the heartbeat 2) Decrease blood pressure 3) Reduce the contraction strength of the heart muscle The effects of these actions are: 1) Reduction of your heart's need for oxygen by reducing the number of times it beats per minute both at rest and during exertion. This is the main way that beta-blockers lower your heart's demand for oxygen, which is helpful in view of the reduced supply 2) Lowering of the pressure your heart must pump against to push blood into the arteries. The lower the pressure, the less oxygen is required 3) Lowering of the squeezing strength of your heart's contraction. This lowers the oxygen use by the heart muscle 4) Lowering of blood pressure in people with hypertension 5) Helping normalize some types of fast or irregular heart rhythms	Propranolol Metoprolol Nadolol Atenolol Acebutolol Betaxolol Labetalol Penbutolol Pindolol Timolol Carteolol (tablets, capsules) Bisoprolol Sotalol	*Inderal* *Lopressor* *Corgard* *Tenormin* *Sectral* *Kerlone* *Normodyne* *Trandate* *Levatol* *Visken* *Blocadren* *Cartrol* *Zebeta* *Betapace*	Prevent angina attacks Lower blood pressure Slow or convert fast heart rhythms Lower risk of second heart attack Protect aorta	Swallow tablet at prescribed dose and schedule	Abnormal slowing of the heartbeat Fatigue or weakness Lower sexual ability Lightheadedness Restless sleep Depression	Asthma, bronchitis, emphysema: may provoke wheezing and breathlessness Claudication: may worsen circulation Heart failure: may worsen heart pumping strength and provoke shortness of breath and edema Diabetes: may lower blood glucose (sugar) or make hypoglycemic episodes (insulin reactions) harder to detect and respond to
	Intravenous: Propranolol Metoprolol Atenolol Esmolol	*Inderal* *Lopressor* *Tenormin* *Brevibloc*	Rapid control of high blood pressure Rapid control of fast heartbeats To continue beta-blocker in hospitalized patient who cannot take medication by mouth For early treatment of heart attack, to lower chances of further damage	Administered by vein		Same as above

This list is not comprehensive and does not represent an endorsement of any product listed.

MEDICATIONS FOR ANGINA PECTORIS: CALCIUM CHANNEL BLOCKERS
TABLE G

Medication and Action	Generic Name	Examples of Brand Names	Uses	How Taken	Specific Side Effects	Specific Precautions
Calcium Channel Blockers The calcium blockers all inhibit the ability of calcium to enter heart muscle and blood vessel muscle cells.	Verapamil	*Calan* *Isoptin* *Verelan*	Prevent angina attacks Lower blood pressure Slow or normalize certain fast heart rhythms	Swallow tablet at prescribed dose and schedule	Excessive slowing of heartbeat Excessive lowering of blood pressure Congestive heart failure if heart contractions already weak Constipation	Caution in people with: Abnormally slow heartbeat Weakened heart contraction Low blood pressure Interactions with other medications
This results in the following effects (although each calcium blocker differs from the other in how much it produces each effect):	Verapamil (intravenous)	*Calan* *Isoptin*	Urgent control of certain rapid heart rhythms	Given by vein	Same as above	Same as above
1) Reduction in the heart rate, thus reducing the demand for oxygen 2) Lowering of	Nifedipine	*Procardia* *Adalat*	Prevent angina attacks Lower blood pressure	Swallow tablet at prescribed dose and schedule	Excessive lowering of blood pressure Headache Leg edema Flushing sensation	Caution if blood pressure is low Interactions with other medications
the squeezing strength of the heart's contraction. This lowers the oxygen use by the heart muscle	Nicardipine	*Cardene*	Prevent angina attacks Lower blood pressure	Swallow tablet at prescribed dose and schedule	Excessive lowering of blood pressure Headache Leg edema Flushing sensation	Caution if blood pressure is low Interactions with other medications
3) Decreasing of blood pressure and the resistance to blood flow through the arteries.	Diltiazem	*Cardizem* *Dilacor*	Prevent angina attacks Lower blood pressure	Swallow tablet at prescribed dose and schedule	Excessive lowering of blood pressure Excessive slowing of heartbeat Rash	Caution if blood pressure is low Interactions with other medications
This makes the heart's task of pumping blood easier and reduces its need for oxygen	Isradipine Mibefradil	*DynaCirc* *Posicor*	Prevent angina attacks Lower blood pressure	Swallow capsule at prescribed dose and schedule	Excessive lowering of blood pressure Headache Leg edema Flushing sensation	Caution if blood pressure is low Interactions with other medications
4) Dilation of coronary arteries so that blood flow is enhanced. This increased the amount of oxygen delivered to heart muscle	Felodipine	*Plendil*	Prevent angina attacks Lower blood pressure	Swallow tablet at prescribed dose and schedule	Excessive lowering of blood pressure Headache Flushing sensation Fast heartbeat Leg edema	Caution if blood pressure is low Interactions with other medications

MEDICATIONS FOR ANGINA PECTORIS: CALCIUM CHANNEL BLOCKERS

TABLE G *(continued)*

Medication and Action	Generic Name	Examples of Brand Names	Uses	How Taken	Specific Side Effects	Specific Precautions
5) Helping normalize some types of fast or irregular heart rhythms	Bepridil Amlodipine Nisoldipine	*Vascor* *Norvasc* *Sular*	Prevent angina attacks Lower blood pressure Lower blood pressure	Swallow tablet at prescribed dose and schedule	Excessive lowering of blood pressure Headache Nervousness, tremor Nausea Rhythm problems	Caution if blood pressure is low

This list is not comprehensive and does not represent an endorsement of any product listed.

MEDICATIONS FOR HEART ATTACK

TABLE H

Medication and Action	Generic Name	Examples of Brand Names	Uses	How Taken	Specific Side Effects	Specific Precautions
Thrombolytics Thrombolytic agents are medications that promote the dissolving of clots	Urokinase Tissue Plasminogen Activators	*Abbokinase*	Dissolve clots in arteries to the lung (pulmonary embolism) Dissolve clots in coronary arteries during heart attack	Given by vein	Bleeding, including internal bleeding, bleeding into brain, bleeding from sites of injury or incisions	Avoid if recent injury or operating, bleeding tendency, severe high blood pressure
They are used to restore blood flow through vessels that are obstructed by a blood clot (thrombus)	Alteplase Reteplase Tenecteplase	*Activase* *Retavase* *TNK*	Same as above	Given by vein	Same as above	Same as above
	Streptokinase	*Kabikinase*	Same as above	Given by vein	Same as above and rare allergic reactions	Same as above and avoid if Streptokinase or Anistreplase previously received
	Anistreplase	*Eminase*	Same as above	Given by vein	Same as above and rare allergic reactions	Same as above and avoid if Streptokinase or Anistreplase previously received

This list is not comprehensive and does not represent an endorsement of any product listed.

Which types of medications are effective in treating Peripheral Vascular Disease?

The process of artery narrowing starts at an early age. This process of plaque buildup is generally across the entire blood vessels of the body, and therefore once you have it in one artery there is a good chance there is some disease in the other arteries. This disease can affect the carotid arteries, which are the arteries in the neck supplying the brain with blood. If the blockage is located in the legs, this may result in a condition called claudication or pain in the lower extremities with walking. It may affect the arteries of the kidney, resulting in elevated blood pressure. More commonly, this process also can result in erectile dysfunction.

MEDICATIONS FOR VASCULAR PROBLEMS
TABLE I

Medication and Action	Generic Name	Examples of Brand Names	Uses	How Taken	Specific Side Effects	Specific Precautions
Anticoagulants These medications reduce the ability of the blood to clot. They act by reducing proteins involved in blood clotting (coagulation) or changing the way they function	Warfarin Dicumarol	*Coumadin*	Prevent blood clotting in high-risk situations such as: Mechanical heart valves Dilated cardiomyopathy Atrial fibrillation Previous blood clot problems	Swallow tablet at prescribed dose and schedule	Bleeding, such as: Internal bleeding into gastrointestinal tract Excess bleeding after cuts Increased nose or gum bleeds Bleeding into joins or muscle Blood in urine Easy bruising Bluish discoloration of toes	Use with caution in liver disease. Numerous medications can affect activity of anticoagulants – check with doctor. Need to check blood test (INR) regularly

MEDICATIONS FOR VASCULAR PROBLEMS
TABLE I *(continued)*

Medication and Action	Generic Name	Examples of Brand Names	Uses	How Taken	Specific Side Effects	Specific Precautions
Anticoagulants *(continued)*	Heparin Ardeparin Dalteparin Danaparoid Enoxaparin Madroparin Tinzaparin	*Normiflo Fragmin Orgaran Lovenox*	Prevent blood clotting in high-risk situations, such as: All of above In certain hospitalized, injured, or bed-bound patients In heart attack or unstable angina After thrombolytic therapy Pulmonary embolism Compared with warfarin, begins acting faster when medication is started, and effect ends faster when medication is stopped.	Administer by vein or by injection under the skin Injection	Bleeding, such as: Internal bleeding into gastro-intestinal tract Excess bleeding after cuts Increased nose or gum bleeds Bleeding into joints or muscle Blood in urine Easy bruising Abnormal reduction of blood platelets	Anticoagulant effect must be checked regularly with prothrombin time blood test so that dose can be adjusted if necessary
Antiplatelet medications These medications prevent the platelets from sticking to each other	Aspirin		Reduce risk of blood clots, which might contribute to heart attack, stroke, unstable angina	Swallow tablet at prescribed dose and schedule One aspirin (325 mg) or one baby aspirin (81 mg) daily is generally enough for antiplatelet effects	Stomach irritation Increased chance of bleeding or bruising	Use with caution with anticoagulants
	Dipyridamole	*Persantine*	Reduce risk of blood clots which might contribute to heart attack, stroke, unstable angina	Swallow tablet at prescribed dose and schedule Usually not used alone; usually recommended with aspirin or anticoagulant	Upset stomach Increased chest pain Dizziness	

183

MEDICATIONS FOR VASCULAR PROBLEMS
TABLE I *(continued)*

Medication and Action	Generic Name	Examples of Brand Names	Uses	How Taken	Specific Side Effects	Specific Precautions
Antiplatelet medications *(continued)*	Clopidogrel	*Plavix*	Reduce risk of blood clots which might contribute to heart attack, stroke, unstable angina	Swallow tablet at prescribed dose and schedule	Stomach upset Bleeding	Need to check blood test (CBC)
	Ticlodipine	*Ticlid*		Swallow tablet at prescribed dose and schedule	Diarrhea Rash	
Hemorrheologic agents This type of medication is intended to affect the way blood flows by decreasing its viscosity ("thickness") and by making red blood cells more flexible. The effect is to make the blood flow through blocked and narrowed vessels more easily	Anagrelide	*Agrylin*		Swallow capsule at prescribed dose and schedule	Headache Diarrhea	
	Pentoxifylline Cilostazol	*Trental* *Pletal*		Swallow tablet at prescribed dose and schedule	Diarrhea Rash	

This list is not comprehensive and does not represent an endorsement of any product listed.

What's the likelihood of grapefruit juice interacting with medications?

Over the past 15 years, there has been a great deal of research dealing with the mechanism and consequences of drug interaction with grapefruit juice. Several hundred publications have appeared in the scientific literature.

When we take medications, they eventually are metabolized in the gastrointestinal system. Grapefruit juice contains a number of natural substances that may inhibit the metabolism of the medications and thus may increase the level of medications in the blood.

This interaction is only possible when the medication is taken orally. Intravenous administrations will not interact with the grapefruit juice.

The magnitude of a drug interaction is different from drug to drug even if drugs are in the same class. For example, the lipid-lowering medications lovastatin and simvastatin will significantly interact with grapefruit juice, whereas others like pravastatin and fluvastatin have minimal interaction, if any. Individual variability is also a problem since it is unpredictable. The drug interaction with grapefruit juice usually will occur after a single exposure, for example to a single 8-ounce glass. If the grapefruit juice is taken repeatedly, there is evidence to show that that will worsen the problem.

Likely, although some drugs are affected by the interaction with grapefruit juice, most medications are not. There is always an alternative medication which could be used with each drug class that allows appropriate treatments to proceed safely.

A summary of known and anticipated drug interactions with grapefruit juice is presented on the next page.

This list is not comprehensive and does not represent an endorsement of any product listed.

MEDICATION INTERACTION WITH GRAPEFRUIT JUICE
TABLE J

MEDICATION		MAGNITUDE OF INTERACTION	
	Large	*Moderate*	*Small or negligible*
Calcium Channel Antagonists		Felodipine Nicardipine Nifedipine Nimodipine Nisoldipine Isradipine	Amlodipine Diltiazem Verapamil
HMG-CoA reductase inhibitors (statins)	Lovastatin Simvastatin	Atorvastatin Cerivastatin	Fluvastatin Pravastatin
Immunosuppressants		Cyclosporine Tacrolimus Sirolimus	
Sedative-hypnotic and anxiolytic agents	Buspirone	Triazolam Midazolam Diazepam Zaleplon	Alprazolam Clonazepam Zolpidem Temazepam Lorazepam
Other psychotropic agents		Carbamazepine Trazodone Nefazodone Quetiapine	SSRI antidepressants Clozapine Haloperidol
Antihistamines	Terfenadine Astemizole	Loratadine	Fexofenadine Cetirizine Diphenhydramine
Human immunodeficiency virus protease inhibitors		Saquinavir Ritonavir Nelfinavir Amprenavir	Indinavir
Hormones		Ethinyl estradiol Methylprednisolone	Prednisone Prednisolone
Other medications	Amiodarone	Sildenafil Cisapride	Clarithromycin Erythromycin Quinidine Omeprazole

This list is not comprehensive and does not represent an endorsement of any product listed.

What is the relationship between Cardiovascular Disease (CD) and Erectile Dysfunction (ED)?

Heart disease and *erectile dysfunction (ED)* are a manifestation of the same disease. The major manifestations of vascular disease include strokes, transient ischemic attack (TIA) or a warning sign of a stroke, heart attacks, angina pectoris, and claudication, which is pain in the lower extremities associated with activity.

The definition of erectile dysfunction (ED) is the inability to achieve or maintain an erection that is adequate for satisfactory sexual performance. Erectile dysfunction reportedly affects 10 to 20 million men in the United States and more than 100 million men worldwide. Another 10 million men are affected by partial ED, defined as present but diminished erectile dysfunction. In the United States, about half a million patients survive a heart attack annually and an estimated 11 million have a history of heart disease, making the issue of heart disease and erectile dysfunction relevant to many patients. In some studies, 52% of men between the ages of 40-70 years suffer some degree of erectile dysfunction.

Erectile dysfunction has many causes *(see Graphic A)*. As you can see, a majority of erectile dysfunction is linked to vascular disease. 57% of men who have bypass surgery had prior ED documented. 64% of men hospitalized for a heart attack experienced prior ED. **Therefore, ED could be an indicator of systemic vessel plaquing or an early warning of a heart attack or stroke.**

CAUSES OF ED
Graphic A

Diabetes	30% - 60%
Cardiovascular disease (CVD)	70%
Chronic renal failure	40%
Hepatic failure	25% - 70%
Multiple sclerosis	71%
Severe depression	90%
Smoking	30%
Radical prostatectomy (RRP)	57%
RRP, with bilateral nerve sparing	20%
Radiation therapy	35%

The conditions, which will increase the risk for ED, are listed in graphic B. It is often linked to medical conditions, rather than psychological.

RISK FACTORS FOR ED
Graphic B

♥ Hypertension
♥ Hyperlipidemia
♥ Hypogonadism
♥ Endocrine disorders
♥ Smoking
♥ Alcohol abuse
♥ Drug abuse
♥ Anemia

♥ Trauma or surgery to the pelvis or spine
♥ Coronary artery or peripheral vascular disease
♥ Peyronie's disease
♥ Vascular surgery
♥ Depression

Sometimes ED is worsened by the use of certain drugs, the most common of which are listed in Graphic C.

DRUGS ASSOCIATED WITH ED
Graphic C

▼ Alcohol	▼ Beta blockers
▼ Estrogens	▼ Psychotropics
▼ Antiandrogens	▼ Cigarettes
▼ H2-receptor blockers	▼ Cocaine
▼ Anticholinergics	▼ Spironolactone
▼ Ketoconazole	▼ Lipid-lowering agents
▼ Antidepressants	▼ NSAIDs
▼ Marijuana	▼ Cytotoxic drugs
▼ Antihypertensives	▼ Diuretics
▼ Narcotics	

Over the past few years, there has been a great deal of interest in treating erectile dysfunction. As listed in Graphic D, the majority of patients prefer oral medications than other modalities of treatment.

Graphic D

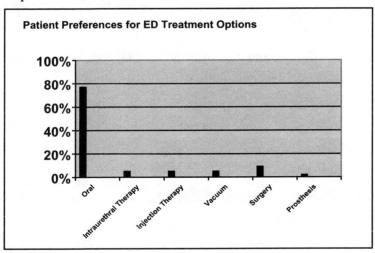

189

Currently, there are three drugs approved by the FDA for treatment of erectile dysfunction, as listed in Graphic F.

MEDICATIONS FOR ERECTILE DYSFUNCTION
Graphic F

Medication	Suggested Starting Dose	Maximum dose	How Taken	Approximate drug half-life	Approximate complete elimination	Side Effects	Precautions
Sildenafil (Viagra)	50 mg	100 mg	Given orally, one hour before sexual intercourse on an empty stomach	4 hours	24 hours	Most common side effects	Use of these drugs in combination
Vardenafil (Levitra)	10 mg	20 mg	Given orally, one hour before sexual activity Avoid high-fat meals when taking it	4 hours	24 hours	are headache, flushing,	with nitroglycerin products is contraindicated.
Tadalafil (Cialis)	10 mg	20 mg	Given orally, one hour before sexual activity	17 hours	3 days	nausea, rash, nasal congestion, abnormal vision, dizziness, diarrhea, muscle and back ache	This may results in a life-threatening condition. Consult your physician about drug interactions

Consult your physician before taking any of the above medications
This list is not comprehensive and does not represent an endorsement of any product listed.

Before taking medication for ED, you should consult your physician, especially if you have three or more risk factors, including documented history of heart disease, symptoms of angina, and conditions such as uncontrolled elevation of blood pressure, significant arrhythmias, or heart valve disease.

Finally, there is evidence that sexual activity actually may prolong life. In a published study, the orgasmic frequency resulted in a decrease in death due to heart disease.

 *Chapter 16*

Heart Tests You Need to Know

Rafat Padaria, MD

What is an exercise stress test?

An *exercise stress test* helps to determine if blockages exist in the arteries of the heart. A narrowing in those arteries can cause lack of blood supply to the heart, particularly when the heart is under stress. A stress test simulates physical stress and allows the physician to determine whether a narrowing exists in the coronaries.

During a stress test, the *electrocardiogram (ECG)* monitors the electricity of the heart. If blood supply under stress is insufficient, the ECG will generally show characteristic changes that can allow the doctor to conclude whether blockages exist or not.

What types of stress tests are there?

There are many ways of stressing the heart. This can be performed by a treadmill (*treadmill stress test*) or by medications (*pharmacologic stress test*). The two most common medications used for pharmacologic stress testing are *adenosine* and *dobutamine*.

Irrespective of how the heart is stressed, the reaction of the heart under stress can be monitored by several ways: observing the ECG changes, or by taking pictures of the heart

191

immediately after the stress test using a ***nuclear camera*** or an ***ultrasound machine (Echocardiogram)***.

What is a treadmill stress test?

A ***treadmill stress test*** involves stressing the heart by having the patient exercise on a treadmill. By using different grades of elevation and speeds at regular time intervals, the heart will be subjected to a monitored stress. The higher the heart rate and blood pressure during stress, the more stress the heart will be subjected to. In order for the test to be meaningful, patients should exercise to at least 85% of the maximum predicted heart rate for their age calculated by ([220-age]x 85%)

A ***regular treadmill stress test*** involves only monitoring the ECG during stress. Unfortunately this test can carry a 20-30% risk of false normal or false abnormal readings and might not be always accurate. However, a lot of information can be obtained from this test, as indicated below.

What information can be obtained from a regular treadmill stress test?

The exercise stress test may reproduce the symptoms of a patient such as shortness of breath or chest pain. This can be helpful to determine whether these symptoms are exertional or random. ***Exertional symptoms*** (that is, those that occur during exercise) are more likely to be related to the heart.

Also, the ECG may show changes suggestive of blockages in the heart arteries or rhythm problems.

Furthermore, the blood pressure response to exercise

will show if a patient is responding appropriately to exercise or has poorly controlled high blood pressure. Finally, *functional capacity* or *conditioning* can be assessed from an exercise treadmill test. This latter is the most important information generated by a stress test since it can predict patient prognosis. In other words, if patients meet a good functional capacity during the stress test, their risks are generally low for cardiac events for 2 to 4 years after the stress test.

It is important to know that a stress test does not predict a heart attack. Heart attacks can happen in blockages less than 50% in severity (typically requires no mechanical treatment such as surgery or angioplasty). These blockages do not show up on a stress test. It is important for patients with normal stress tests to continue to aggressively modify their risk factors, such as by lowering high blood pressure, cholesterol or blood sugar if diabetic, as well as quitting smoking, exercising, eating a low-fat diet and reducing stress.

What is a nuclear stress test?

The *nuclear stress test* is similar to the exercise stress test but in addition evaluates blood flow to the heart and assesses heart pump function. In other words, during a nuclear stress test, pictures of the heart are taken in addition to interpreting the ECG. The nuclear stress test is more expensive than the regular stress test but also provides more accurate information about the heart. The nuclear stress test still, however, carries a 15-20% chance of a false abnormal or normal test.

How is a nuclear stress test performed?

A *nuclear stress test* is performed by injecting a radioactive substance in the arm vein immediately after exercise or while stressing the heart with medications. The patient is then placed under a camera and images are obtained. This takes about 30 minutes. Repeat images are obtained by injecting the radioactive agent at rest as well, generally the next day. The 2 sets of images are compared to each other to look for any areas of reduced blood flow to the arteries of the heart during the stress. If blood flow to the heart is seen during the stress part of the stress test and not during the rest part, this usually indicates the presence of a blockage in the coronaries.

Are there any side effects of the drugs used to stress the heart?

The drugs commonly used to stress the heart are either dobutamine or adenosine.

Dobutamine, which stresses the heart by increasing heart rate and contraction of the heart, can cause a fluttering in the chest as heart rate increases. Also some patients might experience a headache or nausea from the medicine. Patients also can report chest pain and shortness of breath. All these symptoms usually resolve within 5-10 minutes of stopping the infusion of the medication.

Adenosine stresses the heart by diverting blood away from a narrowed area in the coronaries worsening the lack of blood supply to this area. During the 4- to 6-minute infusion, patient heart rate can slow down. Also patients might feel nausea, headaches, shortness of breath, flushing and chest pain. Adenosine lasts only for few seconds in the body after the infusion is terminated. Symptoms usually subside very quickly, often within a minute of stopping the medication.

What is an echocardiogram?

An *echocardiogram* is a test that evaluates the heart muscle and heart valves by using ultrasound pulse waves to record heart images, heart structure and heart function. Any damage to the heart muscle or any leakage or narrowing of the valves can be observed by this test. The ultrasound can see inside the chambers of the heart and therefore can detect blood clots in the heart or birth defects.

What is an echocardiogram stress test?

An *echocardiogram stress test* is done in three stages. First, baseline pictures of the heart are obtained by using an ultrasound machine, without the patient being under stress. Next, the patient is exercised on a treadmill or given a medicine to stress the heart. Then, immediately after the stress, pictures of the heart are obtained again and the motion of the heart muscle at rest and under stress is then compared. If parts of the heart weaken under stress, the test will then be abnormal and suggest the presence of blockages in the coronaries.

What is a transesophageal echocardiogram (TEE)?

A *transesophageal echocardiogram (TEE)* of the heart is a technique by which ultrasound images of the heart are obtained by inserting a probe into the food pipe (esophagus) and stomach. The images are obtained from these locations because of their close proximity to the heart. Usually clear images are obtained with TEE. Since this technique is partly invasive, it is done only when the question in place cannot be answered by the regular ultrasound.

During this procedure, the patient is given sedation through an intravenous line and by spraying the throat with a local anesthetic agent to numb the gag reflex. Usually this procedure takes about 10-15 minutes.

What is a cardiac angiogram?

A *cardiac angiogram* or *cardiac catheterization* is an invasive procedure that allows the heart doctor to see the coronary arteries under x-ray. An angiogram is done under local anesthesia and light sedation. A plastic tube (or catheter) is inserted into the patient's femoral artery (located in the groin area). Through this catheter, plastic tubes are directed under x-ray to the heart where they engage directly the coronaries. A contrast dye is then injected into the coronaries and pictures are obtained.

The arteries of the heart are then visualized and narrowings in these arteries are identified if present. The angiogram is often called the "gold standard" to diagnose significant narrowings in the arteries because it carries a high level of accuracy.

The risks of a cardiac angiogram are low in frequency but can increase in the elderly person or patients with heart failure, kidney disease or vascular disease. The risks, among others, can be death in less than 1 in every 1000 people, stroke and heart attacks in less than 1 in every 500 people, bleeding, infection, nerve damage, electrical disturbances or kidney failure.

What is a significant blockage on an angiogram?

Blockages are classified as *mild* (less than 50% in severity), *moderate* (between 50 to 70%) and *severe* (more than 70%). After the cardiologist defines the location and severity of the blockages in the arteries, the decision to treat the blockages will be based on many factors. Again, **it is important to note that identifying a blockage and treating it does not prevent a heart attack from happening**. The primary purpose of treating a blockage is to reduce symptoms of chest pain or shortness of breath, assuming there is a high suspicion of a link between a blockage and the symptoms.

What is an electrophysiology test?

An *electrophysiology test* is an invasive procedure aimed at testing whether the heart is at high risk of developing an electrical disturbance. The test is done under local anesthetic and light sedation. It is usually reserved for high-risk electrical abnormalities that are symptomatic or life-threatening.

During this test, the electrophysiologist inserts catheters to the heart and performs a programmed electrical stimulation of the heart. Depending on the heart response to this electrical stimulation, information about the electrical stability or conduction of electricity in the heart is obtained.

What is a calcium scan of the heart?

A *calcium scan of the heart* involves detecting the level of calcium deposits in the coronary arteries using a non-invasive specialized scan. The level of calcium in the arteries correlates with the presence of coronary artery disease. Also, the higher the calcium in the coronaries, the poorer the overall prognosis of a patient. If a patient has an abnormal scan, a stress test is the next step to determine whether it is necessary to proceed with an invasive test, such as an angiogram. In general, the presence of high calcium in the coronaries implies that an aggressive approach should be attempted to reduce traditional cardiac risk factors.

 **Chapter 17**

Learn What to Do in a Medical Emergency

Penny Stoakes, BS, RN

During a heart attack, every minute counts – so recognizing the symptoms of a heart attack and seeking medical help can greatly improve your chances for a good recovery.

Let's review exactly what a heart attack is. A ***heart attack*** happens when a blocked blood vessel to the heart keeps the oxygen from feeding the heart muscle. Without oxygen the heart muscle becomes damaged. Permanent damage occurs without treatment. A damaged heart has much more difficulty pumping the blood throughout the body, which leads to serious consequences.

During a heart attack, every minute counts!

The sooner you recognize the symptoms of a heart attack and seek treatment, the better your chances are for a good recovery.

Remember: Early treatment minimizes damage.

Coronary heart disease is America's number 1 killer. It is so important to know and understand your **risk factors,** the **warning symptoms**, and **what to do in this emergency situation**.

What is a risk factor for heart attack?

A *risk factor* is a disease or habit that we know increases your chances of heart disease and heart attacks. There are risk factors that you can change and others that you cannot.

What are risk factors that I can change?

You can have a positive effect on your health by addressing the following risk factors:

1. Smoking: The best approach to take care of this problem is simply to QUIT altogether. When you have the desire to quit, your doctor can give you some medications that help, such as nicotine patches or a medicine called Wellbutrin.

2. High Blood Pressure: See your doctor regularly and take your medication faithfully.

3. Cholesterol: Know what your levels are and what they mean. Ask your doctor to check them if you don't know and check them regularly. If you are on prescribed medication, take it regularly and exactly as prescribed.

4. Exercise: If you live a sedentary life, try putting more exercise into your daily routine – even a short walk every day will enhance your feelings of well-being and may lead to a more active life. It can also increase your HDL, or good cholesterol, and help lower your LDL, or bad cholesterol. It can help to lower your blood pressure and even help to lower blood sugars if you are diabetic.

5. *Diet:* After finding out what your cholesterol levels are, take steps to learn about good and bad fats and how to improve your diet to a more heart-healthy one.

6. *Stress:* Stress levels can be changed or at least better managed by educating yourself on what causes you stress and how you can more effectively manage feelings of stress.

What are risk factors that can't be changed?

1. *Genetics*: You can't change who your parents are and what they pass down to you. If your parents have had heart problems, it increases your chances of having them too, unless you educate yourself on how to maximize your health situation and change the risk factors you are able to change.

2. *Diabetes:* Uncontrolled diabetes can accelerate heart disease. Stay on your prescribed diet and medication, check your blood sugars regularly and report any changes to your doctor.

3. *Age:* The older we are, the higher the chance of heart disease.

4. *Gender:* Men tend to have more reported heart disease than women, although new research indicates women have much more heart disease than previously noted.

How do I know if I am having a heart attack?

If you are unsure of your symptoms, always assume it may be a heart attack. Never worry about a false alarm.

A heart attack may be sudden and very intense. Often people will say, "I felt like an elephant was sitting on my chest" and there is little doubt what is happening. But the majority of heart attacks happen slowly, with mild pain or a vague achiness. It can happen at any time, at rest or with activity.

What are the symptoms of a heart attack?

Chest or Abdominal Pain

1. It may come and go, or stay constant.
2. It can be a severe, crushing pain.
3. A tight, squeezing sensation.
4. A stabbing or burning that feels like indigestion.
5. Pain or pressure under the breast bone or in the middle of your back.

Arm Pain – may be a soreness or heaviness

1. Can affect one or both arms.
2. Pain may spread from the chest or stay localized in just the shoulder or arm and not affect the chest at all.
3. Sometimes described as a soreness or ache that people may mistake for muscle strain.
4. If it comes and goes, chances are it is heart-related.

Neck or Jaw Pain

1. You may experience severe pain in your jaw, up your neck or even around your ears.

2. It may be mild or severe and can spread from your chest up to these areas.

Other Heart Attack Symptoms

Symptoms can occur at any time and may or may not be accompanied by the following:

1. Profuse sweating; also may be a cold, clammy sweat.
2. Nausea and vomiting without warning or burning in the throat.
3. Shortness of breath.
4. Anxiety or feelings of doom.
5. Skin color changes – skin is cool and moist, and changes from pink to pale or gray.

The "bottom line" is: If you have unexplained pain or achiness from your stomach to your ears, check it out with your doctor. If you don't have a doctor, the emergency room of your local hospital will find you one, and you will get the care you need.

What is the difference between a Heart Attack and Angina?

Angina (heart pain) can feel just like having a heart attack. Both can be similar. Angina gets better with stopping activity or usually goes away within a few minutes. It responds to the drug nitroglycerin if used appropriately. With a heart attack, the symptoms don't go away and medical treatment is needed immediately.

What if I don't know the difference?

If you are not sure of the symptoms, **always** assume it may be a heart attack. **NEVER WORRY about a false alarm.** Your doctors, as well as your family, would rather you seek emergency care than have serious or fatal heart damage.

What should I do if I think I am having a heart attack?

Call 9-1-1. NEVER drive yourself to the hospital! The ambulance will quickly arrive with trained medical professionals who will assess your situation. They will give you medicine or oxygen that will help your blood vessels and buy you time in preventing heart damage. In the event you should go into cardiac arrest, they are well-trained in resuscitation and can call into the hospital for medical advice.

If you or someone else tries to drive you to the hospital, your condition could rapidly change and you could become unconscious. You must rapidly get to the hospital and get medical attention.

What else can I do to help myself in this situation?

1. Stay calm.
2. Unlock your front door so help can get into your house.
3. Rest in a chair or lie down – conserve your energy and your oxygen.
4. Loosen tight or restrictive clothing.

5. Take nitroglycerin if previously prescribed by your doctor.

6. Wait for help – don't try to drive yourself!

What can I do if I am with someone who goes into cardiac arrest?

1. Check for responsiveness by gently shaking the person.

2. Listen at their mouth and nose for sounds of breathing. Check for several seconds.

3. Check for a pulse – this could be at the wrist (follow the thumb up to the wrist, place 2 fingers gently on the wrist and feel for a few seconds).

4. If you can't get any of these responses, call 9-1-1.

5. Begin CPR if you have been previously trained.

6. Never leave the person if you can avoid it.

7. Call out for help.

What can I do to prepare myself for these emergencies?

1. Take a community-based CPR class; you may someday save a life.

2. Keep an updated list of all your medications, your doctors, person to call in the event of an emergency and the phone numbers in your wallet or purse and automobile glove compartment at all times.

**Remember: Minutes count
when having a heart attack.
Educate yourself on the symptoms
and seek IMMEDIATE medical attention.**

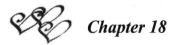 **Chapter 18**

How to Choose Your Doctor and Hospital

Anne D. Pauly, MS, RN, BC

Choosing the right *cardiologist* (a doctor who specializes in the treatment of heart disease) can be a challenging step. Cardiologists are specialists, and the majority of them accept patients by referral from a primary care doctor. Finding the right primary care doctor is one of the best things you can do for yourself. Primary care physicians are the "gatekeepers," referring you to the appropriate specialist, including a cardiologist if you need one. Most of this chapter will focus on how to find the right primary care doctor for you since this step most often leads you to the specialist you need to see.

Finding the right primary care doctor
is one of the best things
you can do for yourself.

How do I find a doctor if I move to a new town, or want to change the doctor I currently have?

First, check with your health insurer or employer's benefits office. Insurance plans are continually changing.

♥ You may be limited to a list of doctors who agree to certain requirements.

♥ One requirement might be that you must select a primary care physician from the list.

♥ This physician is then responsible for your care.

What if my insurance does not limit my choice of a physician?

If you are not limited to a list of doctors, you might want to look in the phone book. Physicians probably will be listed by specialty. You will want a physician who will provide overall management of your health care.

1. For adults, a Family Practice physician or Internal Medicine specialist (Internist).
2. For women, an Obstetrician/Gynecologist.
3. For children, a Pediatrician.
4. For elderly, a specialist in Geriatrics.

♥ A Family Practice physician can usually manage all of the above groups of patients and will refer as necessary.

♥ You might also inquire of friends or co-workers about physicians they like.

♥ Many county medical societies will provide you with a list of family physicians or those with specialties you want.

♥ Hospitals in your area might offer referral services. Check with them.

What kind of doctor should I be looking for?

You will be looking for Medical Doctors (MDs) and/or Doctors of Osteopathy (DOs).

What is the difference between these doctors?

Both of these types of doctors are basically taught
the same way and have their advanced training (residency)
together. The DOs have a little more osteopathic training
(therapy based on the assumption that health can be restored
best by manipulating the skeleton and muscles). MDs and
DOs may be specialized in any one of a large number of
specialties, such as cardiology, gastroenterology, neurology,
orthopaedics, etc.

You will be looking for an MD or DO as your primary
care provider who would then refer you to a specialist when
necessary.

What if I need a referral?

If you need a referral to other health specialists, the
primary care physician must make the necessary referral.

When I have the appointment, will I always see the physician?

Many doctors have other health practitioners working
with them. They may have Nurse Practitioners (NPs) or
Physician Assistants (PAs) working with them.

♥ A *Nurse Practitioner (NP)* , or Advance Registered
Nurse Practitioner (ARNP), is a registered nurse with
an advanced nursing degree, usually a Master's degree.
The NP is also specially trained to diagnose and
prescribe certain medications.

♥ A *Physician Assistant (PA)* is a professional trained in the medical model to assess and examine the patient, perform certain procedures, and give instructions to patients.

The NPs and the PAs practice under the direction of physicians. They may see the patient initially, obtain a history and perform a physical exam. If the physician sees the patient, the NPs and PAs may reinforce instructions from the doctor and/or spend time with the patient answering questions and teaching the patient how they can improve and/or maintain their health.

The NPs and PAs perform an invaluable service to the physician and patient in that they can usually spend more time getting to know the patients, their health problems and concerns than the physician has time to do.

When I decide which doctors I might want, what's my next step?

♥ When you have your list of physicians, from whatever your source – insurance list, friends/coworkers, county medical society – call the doctors' offices to ask if they are accepting new patients and if they will accept your insurance plan.

♥ Keep track of how you are treated on the phone, how promptly you were waited on, and if the staff is willing to respond to a few questions that you have about the care of patients in that practice. If they do not have the time, would they be willing to call back at their convenience? If they don't call back in a reasonable length of time, call back one more time, then consider other offices if they won't respond to you.

♥ If they call back, ask them the questions you might have. If you like what you hear, consider making an appointment. If not, don't call back. Remember, you are looking for a knowledgeable, competent person whom you can trust and who can diagnose and help you sort out your problems and assist in finding a solution.

♥ Before you actually make the appointment, call your county or state Medical Board to verify that the doctor has a current license in your state. Also, find out if there have been any disciplinary actions or if any charges are pending.

When should I make an appointment?

The best for both you and your physician is to meet and talk about your health concerns while you are well. The more you are informed about your health and can effectively discuss concerns with your doctor, the better he or she is going to be able to help you get in shape and stay that way.

When you have decided on your new doctor, make an appointment and have your records transferred from your previous doctor.

What do I need to take with me to the doctor?

There are things your doctor will want to know about your health history, so prepare and take a list with you:

♥ Current conditions for which you are being treated.

♥ Be sure to list and highlight any allergies you have to medications, latex, etc.

♥ Surgeries you have had, and when they occurred.

♥ Things that have changed since the last time you saw a doctor.

♥ Prescription drugs you take and dosages – take the original medication containers to show the correct dose information.

♥ List any over-the-counter (OTC) medications you are taking, such as vitamins, herbal medications, pain medication, nutrition supplements, etc.

♥ Name and address of your previous doctor(s).

♥ Person(s) to contact in an emergency.

♥ Your employer's address and phone number, if currently employed.

♥ Your Medicare and/or insurance company and policy numbers – bring insurance ID cards if you have them.

♥ Family medical history.

♥ If you are of a different culture and there is something specific you need, let your doctor know. Doctors deal with many different people and need to understand multicultural health information.

♥ List any types of alternative therapies you are using (e.g., chiropractic, naturopathic, Reiki, etc.).

What else should I think about before going to the doctor?

You may want to take a list of questions you want answered. This may be a very important step for you.

If you are not sure of the doctor's specialty or special area of practice, ask:

♥ Who covers the doctor's patients when the doctor is not available?

♥ Does the doctor use other physicians or nurse practitioners or physician assistant to participate in your care, and is it optional?

♥ Does the doctor have special training in managing any medical conditions you have, such as diabetes, high blood pressure, heart disease, etc.?

♥ Will the doctor be willing to care for other members of your family who might need a doctor?

♥ To which hospitals can the doctor admit patients?

♥ Are there any restrictions on the doctor's hospital privileges?

Your doctor will want to know about your health history,
so prepare and take with you an updated list
of all your medications, doctors, person to call
in the event of an emergency.

How do I choose a hospital?

Your choices for hospitals may be limited by the number of hospitals in your area, your health insurance plan, or the places where your doctor has privileges.

♥ Ask your doctor which hospitals have the most experience with your situation.

♥ Call the public relations or marketing department to find out how often the hospital performs the procedure in question or treats a certain type of illness.

♥ Contact your insurer, health maintenance organization, or hospital about published reports of results of treatment.

♥ Federal, state, and local governments also collect and publish information about hospital performance.

♥ The Joint Commission on Accreditation of Healthcare Organizations (JCAHO) is a non-profit organization that evaluates and assists hospitals to improve their performance. JCAHO provides information to the public about accreditation status and selecting quality care. Performance reports of accredited organizations and guidelines for choosing a health care facility are available to the public and can be obtained by calling JCAHO at (630) 792-5000, or visiting their web site at http://www.jcaho.org.

♥ Hospitals who are committed to their patients want to know more about the quality of care they provide. They use this information to improve their service. Call the hospital marketing or public relations department for information about patient satisfaction surveys.

♥ Talk with someone who works in the hospital. This information is usually the fastest and best way to estimate the quality of the care you will receive.

♥ For routine procedures, it might not matter which hospital you use.

♥ Helpful web site: A short web site which describes types of hospitals and more questions to ask when choosing a hospital is called "Choosing a Hospital" at http://www.ahcpr.gov/consumer/qnt/qnthosp.htm.

 **Chapter 19**

Medical Research
and How You Can Get Involved

Monica Youngblut, BS, CCRC

Cardiac research is at the core of new drugs and devices that heart patients use every day. Research conducted by clinical investigators and sponsored by industry or the government or various organizations has led to tremendous advances in taking care of the heart patient, preventing heart disease and predicting a person's outcome in the future. Since clinical research is conducted on human subjects, the patient is a critical element in the research process. It is important to recognize the research process and how it is conducted to protect human subjects and their rights.

Clinical research has led to
major breakthrough discoveries
in the treatment of heart disease
over the past several years.

What is medical research?

Medical research (also referred to as a *clinical trial* or *research study*) is a systematic approach to test new medications or medical devices to determine if they are safe and effective to use in people. Research studies are also done on drugs or devices that are already approved for use to see if there are new ways to use them. We can also observe the long-term effects of these drugs or devices on people who receive them. A clinical research study always has a question relevant to the care of the patient that needs to be answered, and this is accomplished by conducting the study.

Who decides to conduct a research study?

Certain physicians and researchers (also called *clinical investigators* or *physician-scientists*) are actively involved in conducting and supervising the clinical research process. Companies that make drugs and devices conduct studies to have their products approved for use. Valuable information is gained regarding the risks and side effects of the drug or device being tested. This information helps physicians know how to use the drug or device once it is available on the market.

Who approves new drugs or devices to use in the United States?

The *Food and Drug Administration (FDA)* carefully monitors all clinical trials conducted in the United States. The FDA observes for events during a trial that may have caused harm. They decide at the end of the trial if the drug or device is safe for the general public. If so, it becomes approved and available for physicians to prescribe for their patients.

Who pays for these studies to be done?

Trials may be funded by pharmaceutical or device companies, physicians, hospitals or foundations. Federal agencies such as the National Institutes of Health (NIH) or the Department of Veterans Affairs (VA) also sponsor research studies.

Why is research important for heart patients?

Clinical research has led to major breakthrough discoveries in the treatment of heart disease over the past several years. Improved *pacemakers*, *defibrillators*, *stents* and *balloon angioplasty* and a multitude of *drugs* and *devices* that heart patients use every day are the results of long years of clinical research. On average, it takes at least 6 to 8 years to get a drug or device approved for marketing. The cost to get just one drug or device tested and approved can range from several hundred millions of dollars up to a billion dollars.

A clinical research study
always has a question
relevant to the care of the patient
that needs to be answered....

Why would I want to participate in a research study?

By participating in a research study, you may have access to newer drugs and devices before they are released to the general public. You also may have more frequent medical care and assessments as part of participating in the trial. The knowledge that the researchers gain from the trial may benefit patients in the future. There is no guarantee, however, that benefit is an end result of a study.

What are the different phases of research trials?

There are 4 different phases of research trials:

Phase I – These trials are the first time a drug or device is used in people. It is often a healthy volunteer who tests the safety and monitors for side effects. Usually a small number of people (25-75) are involved.

Phase II – These trials involve more people (100-200) than Phase I trials. The purpose is to see if the drug or device is safe and effective. These trials are done before the FDA gives approval for general use.

Phase III – These trials further study the effectiveness of the drug or device in large groups of people (1000-3000). These studies are also done before the drug or device has been given approval by the FDA. Positive results of these trials typically allow a company to obtain approval for a drug or device to be released to the general public.

Phase IV – These studies are done after a drug or device has been approved and marketed. These studies provide more information about how the drug or device reacts in the general population. It also provides more information on the risks and benefits. There may be thousands of patients involved in Phase IV trials.

What is a research protocol?

A *research protocol* is like the recipe book for conducting a research study. It contains information about who may be included in the study, what procedure will be done during participation, which medications are involved and how long people will participate. The protocol is written so researchers at many different places are conducting the study the same way so results can be looked at together.

What is informed consent?

Informed consent is the process of learning about the specifics of what is involved in participating in a research study. The study doctor or nurse will explain what the study is about, risks and benefits, procedures involved, how long the study lasts and what alternative options are available. This information is also provided as a written document that the patient must sign to be included in the study. Patients receive a signed copy to take home and refer to during the trial.

How do I know my safety is being protected?

Research studies must follow federal regulations designed to protect the safety of patients. Most research studies also need to be reviewed by an *Institutional Review Board*, a group of people who review and approve a research study. Their main purpose is to protect the safety and welfare of the patients involved.

What is a placebo?

A *placebo* is a substance that does not have an active ingredient in it that would produce a physical effect. It cannot be used to treat a medical condition. In some research studies, a placebo may be given to one group of participants to compare to the group taking the active medication. Researchers are able to compare the placebo group to the treatment group to see if the treatment is beneficial.

What if I am in a clinical trial and decide I want to stop participating?

At any time during a trial you may choose to withdraw. Simply let the research doctor or nurse know you want to discontinue participation in the trial. If possible, let the research staff know your reasons for discontinuing your involvement in the trial.

What kinds of questions should I ask my doctor before deciding to participate in a clinical trial?

You should be informed of all aspects of a clinical trial before you decide to participate. Some of the questions you may want to ask are:

- ♥ Why is the study being done?
- ♥ Why do they believe this treatment will be effective?
- ♥ Which tests or procedures do I need to have done?
- ♥ What are the risks of being in the study?
- ♥ How long will I be involved in the study?
- ♥ Will it cost me anything to participate?
- ♥ Will I be compensated?

♥ May I discontinue my involvement at any time?

♥ Will I find out the results at the end of the trial?

How can I find out more about participating in a clinical trial?

Ask your doctor if he or she is participating in any research studies for which you may qualify. Check out the Internet for local hospital or clinic Web sites that conduct clinical trials.

 **Chapter 20**

Taking the Next Step – A Few Community Resources to Help You Live More Healthfully

Suzanne M. Hartung, BA

Now that you've read (or at least skimmed!) these materials from medical professionals and you're motivated to make some changes so that you can live a more healthful and fulfilling life, what's the next step?

We've outlined in this chapter some simple *(well, "simple" as in "basic," not necessarily "easy"!)* steps we all can take. Then we profile several community groups that are focused on helping community members live longer, more healthful lives.

What Steps Can I Take on My Own to Live a More Heart-Healthy Life?

1. **Commit to your own well-being.** Chances are that you are involved in helping others lead happy, healthful and productive lives but that you pay little attention to your own well-being. Now's the time to take just a little of that energy that you've been giving to others and focus on yourself, as well. Both you and your loved ones will benefit when you are healthier and happier.

222

2. **Don't smoke.** If you currently smoke, stop . . . there are plenty of self-help materials and products, as well as support groups, available to boost your resolve.

3. **Get moving!** Try to exercise at least 30 minutes a day for at least 5 days per week. If you can do more than that, great – do it! If, however, you can't do that much, do what you can. *Any type of movement is better than none*, and it's a step in the right direction. And the results of exercise – both physical and emotional – are great.

4. **Eat healthfully.** This doesn't mean you're restricted to twigs and berries . . . there are many tasty, healthful foods available these days, and there are plenty of resource people available to help you. Start with your local supermarket – ask to speak with the nutritionist or dietitian on staff.

5. **Maintain a healthy weight.** If, like this author, you engage in a daily struggle with your weight, try to keep your focus on eating the right foods in moderation and engaging in as much exercise as you can tolerate. "Doing the right thing" feels great and is bound to help improve your health, even if you don't see dramatic results right away. *Small steps, small steps . . . .*

6. **Find a doctor who is knowledgeable and approachable and get checked out.** Learn your blood pressure, cholesterol levels, etc. Do what you need to do to decrease your blood pressure, increase your "good" cholesterol and decrease your "bad" and "ugly" cholesterols. If you learn of other health challenges you are experiencing, work with your doctor to develop a

plan to address these issues, as well. ***View your doctor as your professional consultant and partner – you're in charge, and he or she will help you meet your goals.***

7. **Learn the symptoms for heart attack and stroke.** See Chapter 17 for heart attack symptoms and Chapter 6 for stroke symptoms. ***Bottom line: if you are unsure of your symptoms, trust your instincts, call 9-1-1 and get to the hospital.***

8. **Learn what to do if you suspect you're having a heart attack or stroke.**
   During a heart attack or stroke, ***every minute counts!*** Learn these basic principles and follow them:
   • If you are unsure of your symptoms, always assume it may be a heart attack or stroke. Never worry about a false alarm.
   • Call 9-1-1. Never driver yourself or someone else to the hospital.
   • Keep an updated list of all your medications, doctors, and the person to call in the event of an emergency in your wallet or purse and automobile glove compartment at all times.

9. **Seek medical attention promptly if experiencing foot pain at night, along with discomfort in your calves when walking a short distance.**

10. **Reduce and manage stress.** The pace of life today is very hectic. It's heartening *(pun definitely intended!)* to see people starting to take control of their lives, reviewing and redefining their priorities, living more simply. Of course, this is not as easy as it sounds,

but those who practice it say it has changed their lives. Examine your routines to see how you can live a less hectic, more comfortable life. Your health will be enhanced and you will find a greater enjoyment in your life.

What are some local organizations that can be a resource to people wanting to live more heart-healthy lives?

There are many organizations in the Quad City area that are designed to promote healthful living. We are spotlighting four of them in this chapter: the *Quad-City Health Initiative (QCHI)*, the *American Heart Association (AHA)*, the *Quad City Medical Society (QCMS)*, and the *Midwest Cardiovascular Research Foundation (MCRF)*.

We encourage you to explore these organizations if you are interested. There also are many other fine organizations in the area. For details, check the **United Way InfoLINK** Website, www.infoLINK@unitedwayqc.org, or call **2-1-1** from anywhere in Iowa, **563.355.9900** (local), or **888.680.info** (or **888.680.4636**) toll-free.

What is the Quad-City Health Initiative (QCHI)?

The *Quad-City Health Initiative (QCHI)* is a community partnership that seeks to improve the health and overall quality of life in the Quad Cities. QCHI's definition of a healthy community includes all aspects of our region's physical, mental, economic, social and environmental health, including issues of access, affordability and quality. QCHI works with over 120 organizations and 400 volunteers in the Quad Cities area to raise awareness of health issues, create programs to address gaps in health services and foster community collaboration in all aspects of health.

The QCHI emerged out of the interest of community members and leaders in improving the health of the Quad City region. In 1999, the QCHI established a community board, including now 35 representatives of local health departments, providers, insurers, social service agencies, educators, businesses, media, law enforcers, foundations and governments. The QCHI Board meets regularly under the chairmanship of Dr. Richard L. Phillis, MD (Ret.), to establish and support health-related community projects.

Major financial support of the Quad City Health Initiative is currently provided by the generous direct and in-kind contributions of Genesis Health System, Trinity Regional Health System and Royal Neighbors of America. For more information, please visit our website at **www. qchealthinitiative.org**.

What does the Quad City Health Initiative have to do with me?

You may know the Quad City Health Initiative by the projects they support in the community. To date, the QCHI has led and/or partnered in projects to address access to dental care, diet and exercise patterns, heat-related illness prevention, access to children's health insurance, tobacco use, and teenage pregnancy. These projects are named the **Dental Care Smiles for All Team**, **Lifestyle Wellness Warriors**, and the **Heat Emergency Task Force**. Our affiliate projects are **Kids HealthNet**, **Tobacco-Free QC**, and the **Quad-**

Cities Coalition on Adolescent Sexuality and Pregnancy. All of our projects focus on meeting the needs of the Quad City community and improving our community's health and quality of life.

Who are the Wellness Warriors?

The **Wellness Warriors** is a team of volunteers working with the Quad City Health Initiative to help support Quad City residents in making healthy choices regarding diet and exercise. The team assembled in December of 2002 and now has 85 members from 60 organizations in our community. The following is a list of organizations working with the Wellness Warriors as of March 2004:

100 Black Men of the Quad Cities
Alternatives for the Older Adult
American Red Cross of the Quad Cities
American Cancer Society
American Heart Association
Boys and Girls Clubs of the Mississippi Valley
Carleton Life Support Systems
Child Health Specialty Clinics
Churches United of the Quad City Area
City of Davenport
City of Moline
City of Rock Island
City of Rock Island Martin Luther King
    Community Center
Cleaveland Insurance Group
Community Health Care, Inc.
Community Members
Davenport Community School District
Deere & Company
Family Resources, Inc.
Generations Area Agency On Aging
Genesis Health Group
Genesis Health System
Genesis Occupational Health
Genesis Plaza Outpatient Clinic
Genesis VNA
Girl Scouts of the Mississippi Valley, Inc.
Gloweb Industries
Hearts of the Quad Cities
Hy-Vee Food Store
Illinois Quad City Chamber of Commerce

Integrity Integrated
Iowa East Central T.R.A.I.N.
Iowa-Illinois Health Solutions
ISU Scott County Extension
John Deere Health
MetroLink
Midwest Dairy Council
Mississippi Valley Regional Blood Center
National MS Society, Greater IL Chapter
Palmer College of Chiropractic
QC Senior Olympics
Quad Cities Wellness & Rehab
River Action
Robert Young Center for Community Mental Health
Rock Island County Health Department
Rock Island County Regional Office of Education
SBC
School Health Link
Scott County Family Y
Scott County Health Department
Trinity Parish Nurse Program
Trinity Regional Health System
Trinity VNHA
Two Rivers YMCA
UIC of Nursing, QC Regional Program
United Way InfoLINK
University of Illinois Extension, Rock Island
County
Wildwood Designs
Work Fitness Center
Y.O.U. Health & Wellness Consultant

What prompted the formation of the Wellness Warriors?

Did you know that more people die from heart disease in the Quad Cities than from any other reason? Strokes, often related to cardiovascular health, are the No. 3 cause of death in our area. The Quad City Health Initiative reported these facts when it conducted a Community Health Assessment of Rock Island County, Illinois, and Scott County, Iowa, in 2002. Even more troubling, we learned that:

- Our rates for death (mortality rates) related to heart disease tended to be higher than the statewide rates for Illinois and Iowa.
- 92% of Quad City adults have one or more cardiovascular risk factors, including high cholesterol, high blood pressure, overweight status, no leisure-time physical activity and/or cigarette smoking.
- More than 25% Quad City adults have been diagnosed with high blood pressure and/or high cholesterol.
- 64% of Quad City adults are overweight and 24% of adults are obese.

These numbers made us realize that heart disease and unhealthy lifestyles are very important issues for us in the Quad Cities. The Wellness Warriors formed to educate the community about these issues and help support Quad Citians in making healthy choices regarding diet and exercise.

What do the Wellness Warriors want to do?

The long-term goals of the Wellness Warriors are to

decrease the percentage of adults in our community who have high blood pressure or high cholesterol and to decrease the percentage of adults and children who are overweight. The Wellness Warriors encourage adults and children to engage in regular daily exercise, eat daily nutritious meals and receive regular screenings for health risk factors. The team of volunteers educates the community through speakers, conferences and walking events, develops new resources to answer your questions about creating a healthy lifestyle and promotes programs focused on nutrition, exercise or health screenings.

How can I be a Wellness Warrior?

You, too, can be a Wellness Warrior! If you want to improve your health and wellness, follow these steps:

♥ *Quit it!* If you smoke, stop.

♥ *Know it!* Know your numbers, blood pressure and cholesterol. If high, get them treated.

♥ *Move it!* Accumulate at least 30 minutes of activity most days of the week.

♥ *Lose it!* Eat well-balanced meals. Reduce calories if you are overweight.

♥ *Check it!* Get regular checkups.

♥ *Chill it!* Improve your mental and spiritual health, and control your stress.

If you have other questions or want to volunteer with the Quad City Health Initiative, please see our web site, **www.qchealthinitiative.org**, and contact our office.

What is the American Heart Association?

♥ The American Heart Association is the oldest and largest national non-profit voluntary health organization in the world. Their mission is to reduce disability and death from cardiovascular diseases and stroke. They plan to reduce coronary heart disease and stroke risk by 25% by the year 2010.

♥ Since 1924, the American Heart Association has funded more than **$1.7 billion of cardiovascular research** in the United States.

♥ The American Heart Association is one of the most cost-effective organizations in the world, providing at least 77 cents of every dollar to research and education.

What is the AHA doing locally?

♥ The American Heart Association currently funds $6.2 million in **cardiovascular research** in Iowa.

♥ A mass **CPR training event** was held in February 2004 at the Isle of Capri Conference Center, Bettendorf, Iowa, at which time 114 people underwent adult CPR training and 170 underwent pediatric CPR training.

♥ **Stroke, blood pressure and cholesterol screenings** with educational videos and materials have been held in the Quad Cities, incorporating parish nurses, visiting nurses association, hospitals and clinics. More than 660 people have gone through one or more of these screenings.

♥ **Acute Stroke Treatment — When, Why, What and How** workshop in the Quad Cities was held in April

2004. Staffs of the surrounding community hospitals were invited to learn how to evaluate and improve their current stroke patient care in treating and transferring stroke patients to the major hospitals in the Quad Cities.

♥ The AHA continues to work with the hospitals in understanding and implementing the recommendations for **primary stroke centers**.

♥ A **heart and stroke survivor celebration** was held in June 2004, at which time survivors shared their stories and helped bring greater awareness about heart disease and stroke.

♥ The local AHA coordinates the annual **Heart Walk** activity and fundraiser. Any Heart Walk company raising over $10,000 is eligible for 8 employees to be trained in the **Heartsaver CPR** or **AED courses** at no cost.

♥ Over 8,000 **school children** were provided with information on nutrition and the new food pyramid as well as on the benefits of exercise.

How can I connect with the local American Heart Association office?

The local office of the American Heart Association is located at 1606 Brady Street, Suite 213, Davenport, IA 52803. Telephone is 563.323.4321; fax is 563.324.3169.

What is the Quad City Medical Society?

The **Quad City Medical Society** is a professional office serving over 500 physicians who belong to the Rock Island County Medical Society and Scott County Medical

Society. These physicians practice in every specialty and are dedicated to providing the best quality of care to patients and to protecting the health of the community. Together the two Medical Societies represent the vast majority of physicians with offices in the Quad City area.

In addition to supporting efforts that will strengthen the health care system throughout the Quad Cities, the **Quad City Medical Society Office**, the administrative office for the two Societies, helps people find the right physician through a referral service and provides information about physicians' primary specialties, medical training, experience and new-patient policies. The office is a resource to people who seek information about area physicians and maintains a current database from which referrals are made. Information can be accessed from the internet at **www.qcmso.com** or by calling **563.328.3390**. The Medical Society is committed to promoting good patient outcomes and assisting people with serious quality-of-care concerns.

The Quad City Medical Society Office provides valuable educational opportunities for physician members of Rock Island and Scott County, working actively to ensure that social trends and their impact on the health of the community are assimilated into best practices. The current crisis in obesity has resulted in serious implications in many areas. Heart disease, diabetes, high blood pressure, and other medical problems have increased dramatically with the increase in weight. Participation in community initiatives that deal with this problem, as well as others, is an important part of the mission of the Societies. Member physicians actively work to strengthen programs dealing with heart health.

In partnership with the **Scott County Medical Society Alliance**, an organization comprised of physician spouses dedicated to enhancing healthcare in the community, the Scott County Medical Society was a sponsor of *Lighten Up Iowa*, a program which informed Iowans about the growing problem of obesity in the state. Recognizing the correlation between obesity and heart disease, SCMS and the SCMS Alliance locally sponsored 33 walking teams for the program by donating a portion of funds for pedometers to teams in Scott County through the *Hermina Habak Lighten Up Iowa Fund*.

Physicians from Rock Island County Medical Society and Scott County Medical Society volunteer their services to assist patients with questions about diverse health issues, including heart health, by participating in the "*Ask the Doctor*" column. Questions are sent to the *Quad-City Times* by its readers, are answered by local physician specialists and then are printed in the newspaper.

Rock Island County Medical Society and Scott County Medical Society coordinate a *Child Health Month Campaign and Pediatric Hotline* in October in observance of Child Health Month. Physician volunteers from the two medical societies answer questions on a variety of topics related to healthy growth and development, immunizations, child care, nutrition, when to call your pediatrician, fitness, substance abuse, and behavioral problems, among many other areas. Family practice physicians and pediatric specialists participate in this effort, taking calls from parents, grandparents, and teens over a three-hour period.

The Societies are sponsors of the *File of Life* program, which provides seniors, at no charge, with kits allowing them to post important medical information on their refrigerator. Medics, responding in an emergency, are able to access vital information about medications or allergies from victims who are unable to understand the situation or respond.

Scott County Medical Society participates in the American Cancer Society *Relay for Life* as a sponsor, and Rock Island County Medical Society ensures that disaster-preparedness systems are in place and that physicians understand their roles in the plan. Through the Quad City Medical Society Office, physicians can be represented in coalitions promoting better health in the community. The QCMSO maintains positions on the boards of both **Tobacco Free Quad Cities** and the **Quad City Health Initiative**.

What is the Midwest Cardiovascular Research Foundation?

The **Midwest Cardiovascular Research Foundation (MCRF)** was established in Davenport, Iowa, by Dr. Nicolas W. Shammas and is a non-profit, public, charitable, 501(c) 3 regional foundation dedicated to cardiovascular research and education. The Mission of MCRF is to "prolong and improve the quality of life in the communities we serve by conducting and disseminating findings of high-quality cardiovascular clinical research."

The explosive knowledge about diseases of the heart and blood vessels has made it difficult for many patients and the general public to keep up with the rapidly changing field of medicine. MCRF provides educational opportunities for medical professionals and the general public alike.

MCRF's vision for the Midwest is a "consortium of affiliate research sites capable of :

1. Developing and conducting large clinical trials
2. Performing regional educational activities for health care personnel and the general public, educating persons on the recognition, treatment and prevention of cardiovascular disease."

MCRF accomplishments include the launching of its educational web page, **www.mcrfmd.com**, that can be accessed by the public and health care professionals to get updated on the latest in cardiovascular research and education. Also, MCRF released *Learn About Your Heart ... Made Simple*, the book you are currently reading. In addition, in July 2004, MCRF released a new book for health care professionals entitled *Cardiovascular Interventions and Practice Guidelines*, intended to give practicing physicians the latest information needed to care well for cardiovascular patients. This book is a summary of the regional convention that MCRF sponsored in August 2004 and will be updated with annual conventions sponsored by the Foundation.

MCRF has already built a solid network across the Midwest with expertise drawn from several regional states. It will be initiating a registry this summer that will track data from thousands of patients from the cardiac catheterization laboratory at the Genesis Medical Center and, in the future, from other laboratories in the region. This database will generate information that will have enormous potential in understanding the effectiveness and safety of procedures currently conducted in the Quad Cities, the Midwest and the United States.

By December of 2004, MCRF is anticipated to have ten staff members to conduct large-scale clinical research trials, to collect and analyze data, and to write reports on its findings. Three independent contract biostatisticians have been retained to compile and analyze data for MCRF. Using the expertise of a local Information Technology company, MCRF built an electronic network via its web page that has the potential of accepting data from our entire region and links participating clinical scientists in cardiovascular research projects. As this network expands, MCRF will expand its facilities and recruit more expertise into the Quad Cities for its headquarters office.

MCRF could not have been possible without a strong belief in its mission by the people of the Quad Cities and MCRF affiliates. MCRF has already received significant support from local, regional and national funders, especially pharmaceutical companies and private philanthropists. Support for MCRF is tax-deductible. MCRF is a non-profit 501 (c) 3 public charitable foundation. For additional information, or to contribute to MCRF, please contact Dr. Nicolas W. Shammas, President and Founder of the Midwest Cardiovascular Research Foundation, at MCRF's office at 563.324.2828, extension 101 or 103.

The address of MCRF is:

> Midwest Cardiovascular Research Foundation
> US Bank, 201 West 2nd St., Suite 710
> Davenport, IA 52801

Thank You

We thank the following colleagues for having shared information included in this chapter:

- ♥ *Nicole Carkner, Quad City Health Initiative*
- ♥ *Sana Harb, American Heart Association*
- ♥ *Cathy H. Whittlesey, Quad City Medical Society*
- ♥ *Dr. Nicolas W. Shammas, Midwest Cardiovascular Research Foundation*

Keep on Moving . . . Today is the First Day of the Rest of Your Life!

We hope that this information is helpful to you and that you will be able to weave some of this information into your life.

It's not just a catchy phrase for greeting cards – today really IS the first day of the rest of your life!

Partner with your doctor and some of the fine community resources available to you.

Best wishes for a healthful, happy, fulfilling life . . . .

 *Chapter 21*

How Much Did You Learn From this Book: Take a Simple Test

Nicolas W. Shammas, MS, MD, FACC, FSCAI

Take a moment to answer the following 30 "True" or "False" questions. The answers are at the end of the chapter. These questions, which are taken directly out of the various chapters, will make you think about some of the important concepts that have been discussed in this book. Circle the correct answer.

Question 1. Heart disease is the leading cause of death in the United States and can start early in life.
True   False

Question 2. Modifiable risk factors for heart disease include smoking, diabetes, abnormal cholesterol levels, obesity, and high blood pressure.
True   False

Question 3. A heart attack occurs only when a blockage reaches 90% or higher inside a coronary artery.
True   False

238

Question 4. Claudication is defined as pain in the calf muscle, thigh or buttocks occurring predictably with ambulation in patients with significant blockages in their lower extremities.

True   False

Question 5. If you have a family history of an aortic aneurysm, further testing can be ordered to evaluate the presence of an aneurysm.

True   False

Question 6. Any new swelling of one or both legs should be evaluated by your primary care physician.

True   False

Question 7. Carotid artery disease is discovered by the occurrence of pain in the neck.

True   False

Question 8. Too much sodium intake results in the body retaining water, which typically makes the symptoms of congestive heart failure worse. A common recommendation for total daily sodium intake is 2000 mg.

True   False

Question 9. Symptoms of congestive heart failure include shortness of breath with activity, problems breathing when lying down, waking up at night short of breath or coughing, going to the bathroom many times at night, swollen feet or ankles, and general weakness or fatigue.
True   False

Question 10. Increased physical activity has been associated with an increase in life expectancy and a decreased risk of cardiovascular disease.
True   False

Question 11. If you have unexplained pain or achiness from your stomach to your jaws, make sure you check it immediately with your doctor. If you are having chest pain, do not drive yourself to the hospital! Call 9-1-1.
True   False

Question 12. The best way to treat a heart attack at present is to open up the blocked artery in the heart as soon as possible using angioplasty. The sooner the treatment, the better the outcome and the prognosis.
True   False

Question 13. A physician should evaluate fluttering in the chest particularly if accompanied by chest pain, shortness of breath and dizzy spells or preceding fainting spells. Patients who experience these symptoms should not drive themselves to the emergency room and should call 9-1-1.
True   False

Question 14. The younger the individual with a stroke, the more likely that a hole in the heart (called patent foramen ovale or atrial septal defect) has been a contributing cause.
True   False

Question 15. Risk factors for heart failure include the presence of coronary artery disease, high blood pressure (hypertension), diabetes, or a genetic tendency. Excess consumption of alcohol and the use of certain drugs also can weaken the heart muscle.
True   False

Question 16. Men are more likely to be told that they have coronary artery disease than women, because heart disease is not prevalent in women.
True   False

Question 17. Lowering blood pressure can reduce the incidence of stroke by about 35%-40%, heart attacks by about 20-25% and heart failure by about 50%.
True   False

Question 18. Infections such as those caused by bacteria can result in valvular heart dysfunction; medically, this is known as bacterial endocarditis.
True   False

Question 19. Increased blood cholesterol levels are unequivocally associated with increased risk for coronary artery disease.

True   False

Question 20. Aerobic exercise, smoking cessation, weight loss, and reducing carbohydrate ingestion all help to raise HDL, the good cholesterol.

True   False

Question 21. The rising prevalence of obesity and sedentary lifestyle are largely to blame for the epidemic of diabetes. If you have diabetes, your risk factors must be managed extremely aggressively.

True   False

Question 22. Women with coronary disease should not take hormone replacement therapy as multiple studies have shown that this could significantly increase the risk for heart attack.

True   False

Question 23. The addition of antioxidant vitamins (Vitamin E and Vitamin C) to patients receiving statins and niacin for high cholesterol dramatically blunts the ability of these drugs to decrease risk for adverse cardiovascular outcomes.

True   False

Question 24. Stroke is preventable and treatable, and the chances of having a severe disability can be reduced if people recognize the symptoms and act quickly.

True   False

Question 25. Transient ischemic attack (TIA) is a short episode, less than 24 hours, of temporary impairment to the brain that is caused by a loss of blood supply. There is no urgency in evaluating TIAs.

True   False

Question 26. TPA is a clot-buster medication that if given within the first three hours of the onset of symptoms through an I.V. has been shown to improve the patient's long-term outcome from a stroke.

True   False

Question 27. Severe high blood pressure in patients with evidence of blockages in their blood vessels (heart, legs or carotids) can also be due to severe obstructive plaques in the arteries that supply the kidneys.

True   False

Question 28. An echocardiogram is a test that evaluates the heart muscle and heart valves by using ultrasound pulse waves to record heart images, heart structure and heart function.

True   False

Question 29. A cardiac angiogram or cardiac catheterization is an invasive procedure that allows the heart doctor to see the coronary arteries under x-ray. An angiogram is considered the gold standard to verify the presence of obstructive plaques in the coronaries.

True   False

Question 30. Fighting heart disease successfully at a mass level requires a community effort and participation to benefit from educational, emotional, volunteering and financial support.

True   False

Answers to Quiz

Question 1. *True*	**Question 16.** *False*
Question 2. *True*	**Question 17.** *True*
Question 3. *False*	**Question 18.** *True*
Question 4. *True*	**Question 19.** *True*
Question 5. *True*	**Question 20.** *True*
Question 6. *True*	**Question 21.** *True*
Question 7. *False*	**Question 22.** *True*
Question 8. *True*	**Question 23.** *True*
Question 9. *True*	**Question 24.** *True*
Question 10. *True*	**Question 25.** *False*
Question 11. *True*	**Question 26.** *True*
Question 12. *True*	**Question 27.** *True*
Question 13. *True*	**Question 28.** *True*
Question 14. *True*	**Question 29.** *True*
Question 15. *True*	**Question 30.** *True*

Index